THE ARMCHAIR TRAVELLER SERIES

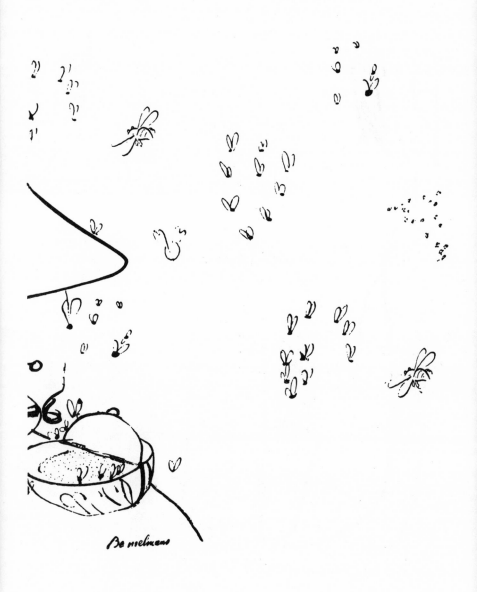

THE
DONKEY INSIDE

by

LUDWIG BEMELMANS

Illustrated by the author

PARAGON HOUSE
New York

First Paragon House edition, 1990

Published in the United States by

Paragon House Publishers
90 Fifth Avenue
New York, NY 10011

Library of Congress Cataloging-in-Publication Data

Bemelmans, Ludwig, 1898–1962.
The donkey inside / by Ludwig Bemelmans : illustrated
by the author. — 1st Paragon House ed.
p.   cm. — (The Armchair traveller series)
ISBN 1-55778-343-8 : $10.95
1. Bemelmans, Ludwig, 1898–1962—Journeys—
Ecuador.   2. Authors, American—20th century—
Journeys—Ecuador.   3. Ecuador—Description and
travel.   I. Title.   II. Series.
PS3503.E475Z78   1990
818'.5203—dc20   89-77910   [B]   CIP

This book is printed on acid-free paper
Manufactured in the United States of America
10   9   8   7   6   5   4   3   2   1

CONTENTS

ILLUSTRATIONS

The S.S. *Mesias*.

"I am only stating that the food here was foul until they killed the cook," said a big man, a Hollander. He turned and, as if it were a rare animal that he wanted to catch without hurting it, he advanced to the rail of the ship with outstretched hands. He took hold of it, held it tightly to test whether it was solid, and then sank his huge body down on it. He was short-nosed, a man with shrimp-colored skin and a pink mustache, and he was drunk. A bottle of Mallorca stood on the table.

A dog came, a mongrel the color of a fox. He stopped, smelled the cuffs of the Hollander's trousers, and with stiff, dancing legs ran away, disappearing around a table.

The table might have stood in the family corner of a third-rate Italian restaurant. It was covered with cracked oilcloth on which stood greasy salt and pepper shakers; a river of red wine, half dried up, wound itself around a vase of breadsticks; and from the rim of a bowl of grated cheese blue flies and little bugs took off, circled under a lamp, and landed again on the neck of the bottle of Mallorca.

Mallorca smells like absinthe. It gets milky when you pour it over ice and mix it with water. It's cheap enough for Indians to buy, and whole villages in Ecuador are in a stupor on Sundays and holidays, thanks to its powers.

The Hollander clasped and unclasped his hands, and sank to his knees between the pink and white filigreed columns that held up the ship rail. He tried to reach one of the six chairs that stood around the table, and fell headlong on a couch whose back rest leaned against a wooden wall of a most beautiful arsenic-green. A decayed awning patched with a raincoat shaded him.

A cow, hanging in a brace of canvas, came down past the awning, and for a while turned in silent circles, its eyes wide with hysteria. Then it dropped in a sudden lurch of a winch and turned again over an old Lincoln touring car. The Hollander snored and the little dog came back. He was surprised by the cow. He stopped and watched it for a second and then he ran on.

Nothing happened but the snore of the Hollander and the take-off of bees, mosquitoes, and small bugs from the cheese bowl. It sounded like a military airdrome, very far away in memory and space.

Down my hand along the little finger walked a fly, a small, common fly with gray wings. She sailed from there for the rim of the cheese bowl and climbed up to its cover. Upside down, hanging from the metallic ceiling, she went along looking for food and stopping. She came to the edge of the lid and walked along it with six legs, I think, three of them on the inside and three on the outside of the lid. She hopped to the knob of the lid, stopped there to clean her wings with the last pair of legs, and then took off again.

With a humming drone she wrote some word in immense letters into the space between table top and awning. The last letter ended up near the raincoat. In the small circle of light over the lamp, like a performer in a circus, up under the roof of the tent, she stood still, and then with the sound of tearing cloth she dived down straight through the narrow space between the glass chimney and the shade, avoiding a bug that came from the opposite side, and soared up again into the warm air and the brilliant light under the lampshade. She gained altitude once more and in two wide arcs shot down into an empty liqueur glass. I thought she would surely crash there, or get stuck in the slush at the bottom of the glass, but she had calculated in millimeters. She almost touched the glass, almost the walls, but in a maneuver too fast for observation she was out and had looped and set her course through the back rest of two bentwood chairs, over my nose, for the shining gold disk in the drunken Hollander's ear. There she stopped to clean her wings once more.

The raincoat patch on the awning moved, a small hairy hand came in, and then a golden eye looked down through a small opening. A monkey, with the motions of a woman taking off a tight dress, wiggled down through a hole no larger than a child's fist. With soft searches, carefully groping with his long legs and arms, and watching in back of him with the tip of his tail, he came down. Grimacing and pulling the skin above his metallic eyes into pleats and quickly straightening it out again, sending furtive looks to left and right, he advanced over the table, stole a piece of sugar without stopping or looking at it, dropped it, and voyaged on to the shoulder of the sleeping Hollander. He reached into the man's pockets, found a coin, stuck it into his right cheek, then went to the man's face, looked into his ear and tried to pluck the small gold disk from it, pulled the lips apart, and examined the teeth. The mongrel dog came on his third round, looked under the table, recognized the Hollander, looked into the kitchen, and ran down the deck, which was split and uneven, like the floor of a neglected bowling alley.

The *Mesias* was occasionally chartered for trips to the

Galápagos. She took mining machinery up the Magda-
lena River, underbid freight rates of the established steamship lines, and was suspected of smuggling gold and helping people arrive and disappear. Most of the time, like a
submerged old woman carrying above water only a garish
hat decorated with banana leaves, she paraded up and
down the coast from Chile to Colombia.

Her crew was half a dozen unshaven men who slept and
drank and sang, and whose brown limbs hung out of the
carcass of the boat wherever the planking was gone. They
lived on bananas, rice, and the fish they caught. The Captain was an amiable Italian with an upper and a lower
stomach, divided by a belt. Since his cook had been killed
he attended to the food himself, and first class were his
spaghetti, risottos, and soups. The Captain's life was made
cozy by an Indian girl, barefooted, with a pair of tinkling
brass anklets on her right foot, and small hands with which
she poured red wine into the Captain's cloudy glasses and
served Mallorca. She smelled of cheap soap, and her cotton
housedress was too big for her: when she bent to serve someone across the table, her firm little body stood in it nude,
with a small appendectomy scar and a medal of the Virgin
hanging between her breasts.

I boarded the S.S. *Mesias* in Arica, a small, clean town
beside a high cliff. The mile-wide cliffs change color from
black to white as the birds fly away from them in an endless
living cloud. They blot out the town, the liners, the horizon,
and the sun. Out over the green waters they drive, in close
formation, their wings touching. It looks as if an immense
carpet with an all-over design of birds were suddenly un-
rolled into the sea.

Hundreds of pelicans in reflective moods line the gunwales of the barges in the harbor. Here and there one sits alone in the water. Seals swim about and play, coming up out of deep water without warning and bumping the pelicans. The fat birds look annoyed, then ruffle themselves back into their dignity and unconcern.

On the day I was on board the *Mesias*, a Chilean boat had caught fire off the coast. The cattle had been thrown overboard and made to swim ashore. (From this disaster came the hysterical cow.) The steerage passengers had been taken off in lifeboats and the first-class passengers in a motor launch. There were only two of these, an American and his wife, and they chose to take the *Mesias* to Callao rather than stay a night at the town's hotel.

They had smart luggage. The man was over fifty, well groomed and elegant—not a businessman. The wife was athletic, gaunt, handsome, and younger.

They seemed very fond of each other, and had great consideration for each other's comfort. The Captain came out of his kitchen and greeted them with his apron wound around the lower stomach. He offered them a drink; the Americans asked for a dry Martini, or some Scotch, but there was only red wine and Mallorca. They looked with suspicion at the glasses with the blue milk in them, tasted it, looked to left and right, and again at the glass, and drank it. "It's very cooling," they said.

The Captain then showed them to their cabin. They came back immediately and wanted to get off the boat, but the two planks nailed together that reached over to the dock had been pulled in, and by bending low or sitting down you could look under the awning and see that the

Mesias was moving out into the green water, toward the endless line of flying guano birds.

The Americans visited the cow on the lower deck. Later they stood arm in arm to watch the copper mountains, and he tried to take some moving pictures. He found the light too weak, but he took one of his wife, anyway. The Indian girl set places at the Captain's table and rang a dinner bell. The American asked the Captain to let him sit at a separate table with his wife. The Captain arranged this. They sat down; he pushed the chair for her, and held her hand at the beginning of the meal.

The Hollander was awakened, and a Frenchman sat down at the table. He was in the diplomatic service and was visiting an oilfield at a place along the coast at which no large vessel stopped.

After the minestrone plates had been cleared away, and the table was loaded with risotto, salad, bread, and cheese, the Captain and the Indian girl sat down and everyone ate in silence.

The mongrel dog came again; the wife of the American petted him and talked to him and offered him food. He ran away on his stiff drumstick legs and continued his parade around the boat. The woman asked to whom the dog belonged.

The Captain wanted to give us some more of his risotto, and the Americans brought their glasses to the table, spilling much.

The Hollander was awake again, and he asked whether anyone wanted some rijstaafel. "Have you ever eaten pio pio?" he asked next. "That's buffalo hide with shrimp. You take the buffalo hide and cut pieces the size of a poker chip out of it, but not quite so regular. You then drop them in hot oil. The basis of this dish is rice also. Have you ever eaten monkey liver?" He turned to the Captain and said that he only wanted to point out that the basis of all these dishes was rice. He fell asleep again.

The Indian girl chased the flies away from him. The ocean was blood-red, the lamp lit. The Captain said that the dog belonged to the cook who had been killed. He waited for a while and looked around for someone to ask him to tell the story of how the cook was killed, and when no one did, he started by himself.

"We were loading cargo in Buenaventura. I was trying to sleep, when suddenly there was a loud scream outside my window, the sound of many feet running past, and much cursing.

"There was a German ship docked not far from us and our cook had gone over to drink German beer. While he was gone we had a visit from a union delegate, a Communist elected by one of the ships in the harbor. We talked about this and that and he had a few drinks here and then he started back to shore.

"Just as my cook comes back and wants to come up the gangplank, the delegate gets hold of him and they get in an argument about the German beer the cook had been drinking.

"The union delegate shouted, 'Down with the Nazis! Down with the Fascists!' My cook said, 'What difference does it make—German beer, American beer, or Jewish beer—what difference does it make?' Diaz—that was the name of the union delegate—pushed him in the face, and as the cook raised his hands to protect himself, Diaz slipped a knife from his belt and ripped him open. We got the money together to fly him to Panama, and there he died. It was plain murder, and that dog that runs around here is his dog. He's looking for him."

The cook's dog had listened to the story and looked up at the Captain, and then had gone on his rounds again, stopped at a dark spot in the planking, and howled out to sea.

The heat of the engine made the place comfortable. Over the swells of water, wide as avenues, ran a luminous band of light to the moon. The sea was studded with the fins of sharks, each one a gleaming, golden plowshare stuck into a black field.

The little Indian girl wound up a portable victrola and Richard Tauber sang *"Dein ist mein ganzes Herz."*

"I can't stand his singing," said the Frenchman to me. "He gives me the sensation of a waiter reaching up under my coat when I leave a restaurant."

The drunken Hollander pulled the Captain's sleeve. "Last time I heard that song," he said, "was in Magdeburg —Malta—well, I am pointing out it was not exactly where the plan says it is. It was in Nell Sprout's, at the end of Kruger National Park. We were coming into the Equator with sixteen parrots and two monkeys; the ship's carpenter built the cages and the Governor of Venezuela came on board personally. I bought some cheese cookies. In the meantime the parrots were dying off. I was married at the time. We had them right there in back of the anchor winch. There were still fourteen parrots and two monkeys. One monkey was dead and the other was dying. They were given a proper burial at sea. The last parrot was buried off Southampton."

The Hollander made an involuntary underslung gesture with his hand to catch his chin and hold his head up. He missed and fell asleep. One after another everyone disappeared.

In the early morning light a fishing boat crossed our course. The Hollander waved to it and climbed over a mountain of cargo to the rear deck, where the carpenter was busy building cages for his animals and birds. The dog followed him there, in advances and retreats, uncertain of his footing but determined to look there too for his master.

In a shelter that they had made of palm leaves, arm in arm, sat the Americans. The little Indian girl came out of the Captain's cabin and stretched herself in the sun in the little piece of cloth that was her dress.

The Americans got off in Callao; the Hollander stayed on, and left with the Frenchman at a small place just before the *Mesias* turned into the Guayas River.

The boat fought upstream half the time, and then ran quickly with the support of the tide. Small bouquets of water hyacinths floated past down to the sea. Dugouts with Indians and half-naked mulattoes and Negroes passed. Large rafts of balsa wood, complete households on them, with children, goats and dogs, ard hammocks, swam along the river. Brown and black legs and banana leaves hung out of boats into the water, out of hammocks, down over bags of coffee; everywhere siesta. In the dugouts were oranges, pineapples, fighting cocks, pigs. Turkey buzzards sat in all the trees along the riverfront. Over the water, and so close that their bellies seemed to get wet, flew trains of pelicans, their wingbeat like a dancing lesson— one, two, three, four, glide. A cool wind came down the river; it began to smell of chocolate. The Captain tinkled his engine bell, and the *Mesias* sighed in a slower tempo, turned, and, between launches that crowded together like young pigs feeding out of the same trough, she squeezed to a wobbly dock and made fast in Guayaquil.

"Stay—today I'll make some lasagna à la bolognese," said the Captain, who never seemed to wash himself.

To the pier came a group of youths and men with caps and rope. Two of them grabbed the lapels of my coat, others gave me a massage; they seemed to have their hands in all my pockets. They all wanted to take my baggage to the Gran Hotel.

I am always unhappy when I leave a place—a hotel, a house, a boat—no matter how bad. For the first few hours on arriving in a new place an emotional sloppiness comes over me; I sat lost and homesick for the greasy *Mesias* in my room at the Gran Hotel. This house, half-garage, half-hospital, is excellently suited to make you unhappy. I went to the dining room, which is on the roof. I tasted the soup and got up and reached for my hat and walked back to the *Mesias*.

The Captain stood in the kitchen preparing his lasagna à la bolognese. In troubled moments there is nothing so reassuring, so kind to the soul, as to watch someone repair something or cook. The Captain oiled the pan with his fingers, carefully placed strips of noodles along the bottom, and spread over them a paste which he had made out of ground beef and pork, some garlic, chopped onions, origanum, and a sauce prepared from Italian plum tomatoes. Over this he put another layer of noodles, and over the blanket of noodles he spread Mazzarella cheese. Then came more paste, another sheet of noodles, and finally he carefully trimmed with scissors the noodles that hung down over the pan and put the whole thing in the oven. He cooked a lot, and he needed it.

2

On a Bench in a Park. In

the morning paper of Guayaquil appeared a small announcement of my arrival. The name was misspelled, but the text was one of cheer, of welcome and enthusiasm over the visit of a "most intelligent and precious North American Author." A picture appeared with the article; "EL SEÑOR BNELEMAAS" was printed under it, and, in smaller type, "Important North American Author"—but it was a picture of James Cromwell.

The reporter who had come to interview me the night before had asked for a picture. I had none, and he said, "All right, all right—I fix it up." James Cromwell seems to be the Ecuadorian ideal of the typical North American. I encountered his picture again in *El Comercio* in Quito, where he appeared as Russell Davenport, another important North American engaged in helping a presidential candidate.

I had hardly cut the notice out and looked into the mirror when a bellboy knocked at the door and came in with a visiting card on a small tray. The sender of the card, he informed me, was waiting for me downstairs in the lobby of the Gran Hotel. The name on the card ran from one edge to the other: "Don Juan Palacios, Conde de Ampurias y Montegazza"; and on the back a few words of greeting were penciled. I was also informed that Don Juan was the historian of Ecuador.

He sat in a chair and around it hung the fragrance of roses; he wore a white rose in his buttonhole and offered a hand cobwebbed with blue veins, the fingers cold and stuck together and the thumb away straight out, a moist, negative handshake. He pointed to a glass: he had ordered half a bottle of champagne. He told me he could read English, read much English and loved it for its economy and precision, but did not speak it; that he preferred to speak French, having spent much time in France, which he loved, as a young man. Since I did not speak Spanish, we agreed to converse in French. "I am so fortunate, you are so intelligent," he said; "I am so glad you have come here. So few Americans speak French well enough to express themselves well. Ah, I am delighted." I bowed, he bowed, and then he offered to show me the city; and he said that he would send me the books he had written, which concerned the city of Guayaquil and the cities of Riobamba and Quito, and that he had also written a history of Ecuador. I bowed again, he bowed again and smiled, the tired smile of an invalid. He then took a silver-headed cane and got up with difficulty; and after this effort, when he could spare breath to talk again, he informed me with a mocking smile that his family was so old and so distinguished that two of his aunts suffered from hemophilia and that his uncle had had a silver hip. We both stood now, and he moved close to me and took my arm; he hooked himself to the inside of my arm with a grip which he did not relax until the end of a long promenade. He wore an old and out-of-date garment, a short coat, once called in France a *pet-en-l'air*, a well-tied four-in-hand, and a collar which in Austria was named *Vatermörder*; his waistcoat resembled the plumage of a starling. He walked with his small legs as if each shoe were a sandbag which he had to pull and then kick forward. It took six separate motions to clear the one step from the

Gran Hotel's foyer down to the sidewalk, a delayed maneuver to turn to the right in the direction of the street. We
advanced slowly past a box of greenery to a sign "Gran
Hotel," to a bell labeled "Nightbell," to another sign which
said "Entrance" and pointed back to the door of the Gran
Hotel; and then came the adventure of crossing the street.
It was done with a waving of the cane, increased pressure
on my arm, and quick breathing. On the other side of the
street he climbed the sidewalk again with great effort and
then stood still. I looked around and was astonished at the
number of casualties in this street: there was a man who
had only one leg; a woman, blind, sat on the edge of the
sidewalk, and a child of about ten had an arm and hand
the size of a doll's hanging out of its left sleeve.

The burdensome parade went on and it had its compensation, for in this retarded progress there was time to see
every detail: the child with the withered arm, the man with
one leg, and the blind woman. I noticed also the great
number of drugstores: we passed three of them in short
order. Most of the medicines in the windows seemed German. On one window a story in pictures was pasted. Obvi-
ously inspired by American advertising technique, this
simple drama was adapted to South American conditions,
in that the man seemed more important to the advertiser
than the woman. It went like this:

In the first picture an old gentleman with a white beard
sits at his window; he is sad. Through the window he sees
the door of a club and two other men enter smiling with
their arms around each other; a third man, also smiling,
waves at them from the window of the club.

Second picture: A kindly friend comes to visit the old

gentleman. He also has a beard, he speaks to him in great confidence, he says some Spanish words into his ear, and the old gentleman listens with surprise. The friend has brought a gift, a cake of pink soap called Lifebuoy. The visiting friend points at the soap while he delivers a long speech.

Third picture: The old gentleman is in the bathtub, shoulders and arms covered with soapsuds, the head and beard now no longer at an unhappy angle. He smiles; the soap is on a chair next to the bathtub and has a few things to say.

Last picture: The old gentleman is in the club, surrounded by his friends with their arms around him. The cake of Lifebuoy soap has a face that smiles and points at the happy ending.

Inside the window of the drugstore are several posters showing people with headaches and malaria; pictures with religious motives advertise aspirin, quinine, anti-flea lotions, and Vicks VapoRub. We went on, and between the last drugstore and a shop for Panama hats and souvenirs cut out of ivory nuts, I saw a large brass plate with the name of a veterinary. I have never heard of one who was better named—it was "Dr. Aníbal Carrion."

Farther on came a film-renting agency, with Shirley Temple, Wallace Beery, George Raft, and Dolores del Rio on the posters that hung over the desks. Down at the end of the street some pelicans went by, and it began to smell of cocoa. Turning the next corner we found the street covered with cocoa beans, and two men, using their feet as plowshares, walked up and down the length of it, turning beans in the sun.

Near the water was a park with several benches, each shaded by a tree which seemed especially trained for the purpose: it grew straight up and then spread like a square umbrella to shade all who sat under it, allowing for outstretched feet and people who leaned back or over the arm rests.

We sat down here and Don Juan pointed at a boat in the river, with a large C painted on its bow.

"That," explained the Count, "is one-third of our Navy. We have three battleships, *A*, *B*, and *C*. This one, *C*, is an old Vanderbilt yacht. It has a bad sternpost but it has six bathrooms and eight open fireplaces, and is the ship most sought after by our officers because it is the most comfortable. You will notice that it has no gun; it had a one-pounder but we took it off because it almost knocked the boat apart when it was fired. The other ship, *B*, is most probably in the Galápagos. We can go to the Galápagos now; we have engaged a man who almost graduated from Annapolis to act as pilot and advise the Captain. Once before, when they went without him, they came back and said that they could not find the islands, that they had disappeared. We had a group of prisoners to send there. The next time we tried with that American, he found them, but that time the Governor of the islands said that he did not like to have the criminals on his islands and they had to be taken back again. Now it is all arranged; he takes them and the boat goes and comes back again and everybody is happy, including the prisoners, who have nothing to do but go fishing all day long. The battleship *A* I have not seen for a long time, I do not know where it is, no one has seen it; perhaps we have only two.

"But look around and you will see many automobiles. When I was very young my family owned the first car here in Guayaquil. At the time it was pure folly to own a car, because there was only one street to drive in and it was not very long, only a few blocks.

"The Americans developed this country. Our car was American. The Americans built the first gas factory here, the locomotives on our railroad are American, the street-cars and the first boat that went up this river, and now the electric works—all American. We are in many ways very advanced: you can have a divorce here for the asking, without trouble, and for a long time, hundreds of years, we have allowed our soldiers to bring their wives into the armory with them, a great improvement on the comforts and the morality of barrack life. Our temperature here is about 79, the dry season lasts from June to December or January, and the evenings and nights are very cool, even cold.

"History—what do the French say of it again?—is a fable agreed upon. Here, the fable is bloody and colorful, with violent incident, with gold, Incas, treachery, and a scoundrel unmatched—at least until recently unmatched— I am speaking of Pizarro. But we also have handy things, lovely memories, good names, and deeds to remember. We are a small country, we have little more than three million people, and the Indians outnumber us ten to one. Most of our people cannot read or write; our records for the most part are unreliable and our statistics largely guesswork."

He was almost serious for a little while. The thin tired smile came again when he said, "We have a revolution

here every Thursday afternoon at half-past two and our
Government is run like a nightclub. We owe some two hundred and fifty million sucres; but who pays debts these
days?"

A man came and offered to change some money—he began by offering the sucre at thirteen to the dollar—but the
Count said, "Wait—let's ask that man over there. Oh, Don
Luis, one minute, please," and while the man he addressed
got up from another bench to come over, Don Juan said,
"He was Minister of Finance in the last Cabinet; he can
tell us all about it." The ex-Minister advised us to change
at the rate of seventeen sucres, and went. "They all fell out
of the fat last week," Don Juan remarked, "and now they
are sitting on the benches in the parks in Quito and here,
and the President is riding in a streetcar. That is democ-
racy."

An old lady and a man sat down next to us, speaking in
French so that we should not understand them. They were
from the Midi, judging by their dialect. The mother gave
her son a long lecture:

"My dear child" (the child was about fifty years old),
"your father and I founded our *affaire* here, thirty years
ago now, in one room; we enlarged ourselves and took two
rooms, then we engaged employees and a few of these are
still with us. We have established ourselves in this place
with a reputation of honorability and honesty, and the
products that carry our name are the best and we are proud.
These Germans offer a good price but if they take over
the business, will they continue in the same manner? We
have gained a fortune sufficient to our simple needs, our

employees are like our children, we are a large family perfectly happy. What more do we want of life? Believe me, my son, let us guard our little house—with our Ideal. Let us be satisfied with that which we possess."

"Do you think Hitler will win?" asked the son.

"Yes and no," said Maman, "but it makes no difference, don't sell the *affaire* now, with the sucre falling, it is now seventeen and might go lower. Makes no difference—like this or like that—what happens in Europe. Here, the Americans will fix it, there will be a conference and they will buy the *chocolat. Cet homme Roosevelt, c'est un phénomène,* wait for him." A young girl with soft blond hair came and kissed the woman, and they got up and walked away.

"Ah, how lovely, how logically, how clearly they can think!" said Don Juan Palacios. "And to hear them talk, no matter what, makes it hurt me here, under my ribs. I become homesick." He looked after the girl. "Did you see her, the blond girl? When I see a blond girl I grow warm like soft chocolate inside—helpless. But one should never bring them here, never bring a beautiful woman into the tropics. Look at her legs! They wear thin stockings and the black flies bite them and lay eggs under the skin, and then it swells up and they squeeze and scratch it and the whole girl is covered with hard red patches, and ruined.

"Ah, but in France . . . You know we love France so much here that at one time the natives and the servants thought that outside Ecuador and Peru there was only France, and the only other city besides Guayaquil and Quito was Paris. In Spanish, 'Frenchmen' is easier to say than 'foreigners,' too, and so all foreigners were called Frenchmen.

"When I was a young man here, I fell in love with a beautiful girl, I wanted to marry her badly, but my father was against it. He went to Quito to investigate her family, and found out that the girl's great-grandfather came as a servant with the first Chiriboga. That was when my family arrived, at the same time as Pizarro, or soon after. Now they are accepted in Quito—at any rate, nobody minds them—but that was four hundred years ago. They even have an escutcheon now; my father almost died laughing when he heard of it. They made a special trip to Spain to establish a title. In those days the King of Spain would hand out papers for money, but he asked too much, and so they came back with a story that the title was there and that they could get it if they wanted to, and they brought along this escutcheon. The father even became President— but who doesn't here? At the time it happened, I was very unhappy. They sent me off to France. . . . Ah, la Place de la Concorde, les Tuileries, the perspective down the Champs-Elysées, the little restaurants in the Bois and in back of the Madeleine! I fell in love. . . . Ah, her little footprints in the sands at Le Touquet! We took a villa in Biarritz—it was covered with a peculiar kind of fawn-colored rambler roses; there were roses everywhere. Suddenly it was all over. I was a madman for a few days, I wanted to die, I was so beside myself that I thought of joining the Foreign Legion and I went there to enlist. It was Saturday afternoon and they told me to come back on Monday. On Monday I felt somewhat better. Ah, Denise,

I have never forgotten her. I had my architect build me a
replica of the villa in Biarritz. It is on my hacienda, up
along the Guayas River. I made the sketch myself, from
memory. I found a man in Quito, with extraordinary talent
and imagination, a Mexican, who helped me with forgotten details on doors and windows and on balustrades. I
watched it grow, and one day it stood there in the true
color and shape of its original. It was raspberry-colored
and covered with roses. We had trouble raising the roses
here; they grow well only on one side of the wall, to the
east—but from there at five in the evening it looks and
smells like France. The sky drawn with blue chalk, the
vanilla color of the doors and the stairs, it is all as it was
and I go there to be lonesome, to feel the ancient ache. I
don't see the wild land at the back of it. When I built the
house, the river that runs past it was filled with crocodiles;
like a raft of old logs they lay there, one next to the other,
and at night their eyes shone. The eyes of the old ones were
red and the eyes of the young ones green. They laid their
eggs on the edge of my garden, and the gallinazos swooped
down and dug them out. They helped me get rid of some,
and the rest I shot, all of them. I made my gardener wear a
big hat and a blue coat, so that he was like the one we had
in Biarritz. . . . I would ask you to come and stay with
me at the villa, but my wife Hortense and the eight children
live there, and it is a madhouse."

We walked back and he promised again to send me all
the books he had written, and gave me a small volume that
he had brought along for me. It was a travel book on
Ecuador, written by Friedrich Hassaurek, who was American Minister to Ecuador, and published in 1867: *Four*

Years among Spanish Americans. I was very grateful for
this gift. I have always tried, when visiting a new country,
to get hold of an old book, because it extends the view, it
helps one to see into the land in much greater perspective,
gives one another life almost—one can look around and
compare and say, the last time I was here this was so and
so. Everything takes on new form and stands out in the
round.

Above all, an old book, written with attention to detail,
is a consolation, a proof that the most important things remain unchanged through all the immediate terrors. Down
over these a benevolent curtain sinks, and on it is painted
the unchanging landscape; it is made up of children, of the
games of children, of cooking, of dances and music, and
the climate; it even has in it the labels on the boxes of food
or medicine, the architecture of a house, words that are
used nowhere else, the sound of the bells of the nearest
church. The storm passes on, these things remain—and
through them we heal ourselves again.

The Count asked me to dine with him, and we wandered
back into the town together. We crept past a row of two-
story houses, most of them wooden, almost all painted green
with simulated marble veins, the upper stories seemingly all
window, and decorated with a kind of wooden lacework. It
was evening and getting cool; we were followed by a horde
of half-naked children who wanted to shine our shoes and
sell us lottery tickets. *"Veinte mil sucres,"* they cried,
"twenty thousand sucres"—the amount you will win next
Saturday if you buy a ticket from them.

We passed a fire company, firemen in red shirts, polished
apparatus, half of them modern and half museum pieces.

"This town," observed Don Juan, "burns down frequently; its history is one of sacking and fires. For a few sucres you can become a lieutenant of bomberos—for a few more a captain, and that entitles you to the pleasure and the honor of appearing in a beautiful uniform, with music, and marching at the head of all the parades and important funerals. But when the city burns, as I have told you it frequently does, you stay home and let the muchachos climb the ladders and run through the streets; that is what they are paid for."

He climbed into a cathedral next, which was built entirely of wood, painted to resemble granite. Inside the church, barefooted Indian fraters prepared the interior for a requiem. Long curtains in black and gold, reaching from roof to floor, were pulled up to cover the windows. Angels made of cardboard appeared and were set to the left and right of the catafalque; a choir practiced a miserere to the accompaniment of an organ; a monk fell off his bamboo ladder and sprained his ankle.

"They love death in this country; it's like a dance to them, they cry for six months. Wait until you see the flowers, the relatives, the wagon with the black angels— and the darkened church. Fires will be lit here and there, blue flames, six priests. It is a wild fiesta of grief. . . ."

I went to my hotel to rest. There was a large bouquet of white roses; the invitation to dine was for nine. I found out in the meantime that here one says "hola" instead of "hello" to the telephone, that while a crocodile in all other languages is a crocodile, in Spanish it is a *cocodrilo;* and that a question mark is put in front of a sentence as well as at the end of it. I found also that the Spanish language is very objective. The back page of the newspaper which I tried to read had a local news report of a tragedy: a young girl had jumped or fallen out of a third-story window. The headline read: "YOUNG GIRL DESCENDS THREE STORIES."

I dressed and went to the address of my friend. He lived in a street of very old and severe houses. A woman in a shawl opened the door and showed me through a long corridor. I passed a second open door, and from the dark room came Don Juan's voice: "Please wait in the next room until I wake up."

A table was decorated with white roses, and fawn-colored ones were in two vases on the wall. A picture of the villa in Biarritz also hung there, a daguerreotype, the sky almost black, the house copper-colored and out of focus, and in the foreground a woman in a large white hat. An old servant looking like a dark imitation of Beatrice Lillie, who was enceinte and walked in large soft slippers, finished setting the table and then Don Juan Palacios came and we sat down. He told the woman to open the champagne. She was afraid of the bottle. He tried it but his fingers were inadequate and then he gave it to me. It was a bottle of Chilean champagne, and though it had been cooled for several hours, almost all of it came out in a high fountain.

The menu opened with some cold hors d'œuvre, things I could not make out, all of them pickled sour things, some like fish, some like meat, including pieces of cauliflower and two slices of beets, sliced onions sprinkled over all.

"You don't have to eat it if you don't want to," said the host, "but I find that of all things of which one is afraid, cold things are easiest to eat: the vinegar is a kind of protection."

A good red soup came next, with eggs and corn in it and large pieces of tomato; then a fish. There came a dish of rice with lamb and cold stringbeans, and afterward a dessert made of pie crust with jam inside of it, and coffee. During coffee Don Juan fell asleep.

3

The Guayaquil and Quito Railway.

To take the train for Quito, you are called at five in the morning, and an old and twisted ferryboat carries you across the Guayas River to Durán.

The traveler here beholds a picture, lit by the rising sun, that is a hundred years old and like the finale of an operetta that has been dressed with second-hand costumes. Only the orchestra, the score for *The Count of Luxembourg*, are missing. Here is a station-master with a coat cut *en taille* and a haby beard. Nuns walk up and down dressed in the colors of several convents, predominant among them the Sisters of Charity of Saint Vincent de Paul, under immense butterfly hats. Between them clatter officers' sabers, hanging from young men of Schnitzler format—garde du corps, Vienna about 1898—their gloves with the fingers almost worn through. There are others, with broader swords, képis, in tight litevkas crowded with frogging—a kind of Hussar. Half a dozen monks, fat and happy, stand talking with folded arms, and aside and serious stands a Jesuit, his eyes on a little book. Commercial people, clerks in bowlers and threadbare black suits, large families with handkerchiefs ready for tears, embraces, and train-whistling, conductor running up and down, salutes and crying and waving of the handkerchiefs.

This train is a curious affair with little wheels and a lid hanging on the side of its chimney. It was manufactured by the Baldwin locomotive works in Philadelphia and the cars that go with it are wooden, red, with elaborate fences around the platform and banisters up their stairs that belong to an old brownstone house. But here is the same train mood as in Victoria Station. It comes from the poom-pah, poom-pah, of the engine, a deep iron breathing and a small mechanical click in between.

An engineer, his face smudged before he starts, looks out of the cab and under the shed that covers the station; smoke creeps along, and the air becomes a kind of champagne for the lungs—carbonated air that makes breathing a pleasure. It expands the chest, one is tempted to cough, but it does not go that far. It is the exhilaration that comes from the tuning of a fine orchestra, rather than from its playing, and it finds its high point in the first two tugs of the engine, when the landscape outside begins to jerk and then slowly move.

Out into the large leaves of banana trees—clatatatat, clatatatat, shaking and trembling and about half an hour late the red train runs. Its most luxurious accommodation is the last car, called an observation car. You can observe out of six barber chairs, three on the left and three on the right, made of genuine mahogany, each one with an immense brass cuspidor next to it, on a green linoleum floor. At one end is a little water fountain, overhead sways a lamp, and in the back through the open door the rails run away and tremble in the heat.

The prospectus of the Guayaquil and Quito Railway informs us that we are in a land of Old World charm, courtesy, and hospitality, a land with a delightful climate to suit every taste, ranging from the tropical to the temperate; that verdure-covered hills are set like jewels among snow-capped mountains; that the distance from Guayaquil (Gwah-yah-keel) to Quito is 462 kilometers; that the railway is the result of the initiative of General Eloy Alfaro and Mr. Archer Harman, a far-seeing North American; that the railway traverses banana and cocoa plantations, coffee and rice and tobacco fields; that the train stops in Huigra and that from there on is the most interesting part of the trip, where the road goes up over the Devil's Nose in a five-and-a-half-percent zigzag and eventually comes to Riobamba, which lies at an altitude of 9020 feet; that the population of this city is 30,000, that it is the capital of the province of Chimborazo, and that it has many fine buildings, parks, statues, and excellent hotels.

The finest of these, recommended to the discriminating traveler, is the Hotel Metropolitano. If you have neglected to order a car to take you on to Quito, this is where you must spend the night.

This violent inn appears to have come out of a story conference of the Marx brothers; it shakes and trembles, it is full of cracks and cold drafts, and the plaster from the ceiling rains down on your face at night. The railroad engines switch cars through its lobby and engineers pull the cords of their whistles whenever they want a package of cigarettes, coffee, the morning paper, or a drink of chicha; the old engines operate with every mechanical noise and chuff back and forth relentlessly. Late guests come in singing, and by the time the last one's baggage is dragged upstairs, a boy calls you and it is time to get up for the second part of the trip to Quito.

The floor is cold, the shoes are outside the door, there is

a washstand under the window, the kind one sees in charity hospitals, made of enameled bent wire which embraces a basin, a chipped pitcher standing under it.

There is of course no soap, and the towel hanging at the side is muggy, gray, and the size of a tabloid newspaper. The boy comes with haste, a cup of lukewarm water in his hand for shaving, and throws the baggage down into the lobby. "*Buenos días,*" says the manager and presents the bill.

The scene at Durán the day before is repeated here with everyone freezing, the officers with their coat collars up over their ears, their hands in their pockets; the nuns are blue in the face. At six, again the train rolls on; here in Riobamba the wind is fresh and the air is light and everything is crisp and clear. The train passes between fields of clover and barley, there is wheat and corn, and Chimborazo appears on the left.

Except for its unforgettable name, it is not a very impressive mountain. It is snow-covered, an immense hill with smooth sides, a fat kind of Fujiyama. A biting wet wind comes down its slopes, so strong that at times it blows mule and rider away. The Indians wear chaps made of sheepskin, they are plump and most of them wear handkerchiefs across nose and mouth. There is dust on floor, chair, hat, and coat, one can write one's name anywhere, and breathing has become difficult on account of the altitude.

Somewhere hereabouts is a watershed—and long before the railroad was built, a Viennese traveler, Madame Ida Pfeiffer, the author of *A Lady's Second Journey round the World*, noted in her diary:

"I got off my mount and climbed a little way down the

western side of the mountain till I came to water, when I filled a small pitcher, drank a little, and then took the rest and poured it into a stream that fell down the eastern side, and then reversing the operation carried some thence to the western and amused myself with the thought of having now sent to the Atlantic some water that had been destined to flow into the Pacific and vice versa."

A little farther on the railroad descends into lovely valleys, into a delicious landscape of geranium trees, of roses everywhere, of white volcanoes, a sort of geological Soufflée Alaska, hot inside and snow-covered outside. The sky is blue as it is in the South of France; it has been described as the land of eternal spring, but it is more like the last golden days of September, and the smoke that rises everywhere on the mountainsides supports this idea—it is like the burning of autumn leaves. All along the way there have been little restaurants—in Huigra is one with a sign that says "Hays Krimm" (Ice Cream) and I have seen others, "Airistiu" (Irish Stew) and "Wide Navel Wiski" (White Label Whisky). These, however, are luxury establishments that cater to the discriminating traveler.

The natives and even some of those who travel first class patronize small itinerant restaurants, places set up beside the train, consisting of a table, a sand-filled box on stilts which serves as the kitchen, and a piece of sailcloth over the whole business. There is a pot for soup and a fire on which the meat is roasted. Chickens and guinea-pigs are cut up with a small hatchet; the cook, in a greasy blouse and a hat such as bricklayers wear, licks her fingers and picks up pieces of meat which she arranges on plates that are wiped but never washed.

Under the oven are several dogs who wait for the bones. The entire personnel of the train storms these field kitchens whenever we stop for a while. A well-dressed man who sat in chair Number 4, next to me, assured me that the food was excellent; he had some roast pig brought to the train and ate it with good appetite.

The engine of the train went for water frequently. Once there was a delay on account of a rail that was loose. Half an hour later the maid of the Pension Hilda in Ambato waved a flag and the train stopped to take on a passenger, who kissed his family and embraced his friends several times, contemplated how much to tip the assembled employees of the Pension, and then discovered that he had forgotten his light green coat and sent the maid, whose name was América, back for it. The green coat arrives after a while—the good-bys are repeated.

"*Vamos!*— Let's go!" shouts the conductor, and the train goes on, over a bridge along a river, over a hill in a sudden wide curve, and Quito is in its embrace.

4

Quito.

Quito, the oldest city in the New World, is seemingly built over a sunken roller coaster. Up and down in wide curves and sudden drops go its streets and white houses; the base of one monument is above the spray of the fountain in the next plaza. It is at once like Tunis and like Bruges, and its near-by backdrop of mountains reminds one of Innsbruck.

I have often expected, at night, that out on the roof of the cathedral, under a foolish golden cockerel that turns in the silent wind, would come Rimsky-Korsakov's star-hatted magician and sing the prologue of the *Coq d'Or*.

It has been said of Quito that it had one hundred churches and one bathtub. There are more bathtubs now, but the churches are still ahead—and they make themselves heard. Their bells are high and insistent; they start ringing for early mass with the crowing of the roosters—clank-clank-clank, bim-bim-bim-bim-bim-bim, bang-bang-bang-bang, and ping-ping-ping-ping. They sound more like large alarm clocks than church bells. The deepest give off a sound like that of a bathtub hit with a sledgehammer; the others are nervous and quick, and none of them has much music— one right next to the hotel goes: "Beany bunk, beany bunk, beany bunk."

In the early Sunday morning hours, when you ride above Quito to the foot of the volcano Pichincha and look down, the city appears as if made of marzipan crawling with numberless black flies. The flies are priests and little women in black shawls running to and from the churches, and in this respect it is like Bruges; but in Bruges the little women walk in twos, and here they walk alone.

The churches are crammed from floor to dome with gold and statuary; their walls are like pages from the Tickhill psalter. The dogs go to church here, they wander in and out, and during the midday heat they lie on the cool floors and sleep in the confessionals. The Indians unpack their children here, sit close together, and everyone prays half audibly—the church seems filled with the flights of bumblebees; fleas hop from one Indian to another. Santa María, Santa María, Santa María, they love the Virgin most and to her they sing and pray, and they believe that a child nursed in church is particularly blessed. They slide on their knees to their saints and light candles and hold their hands aloft in rigid poses of adoration and prayer.

The sacristies are elaborate apartments, filled with statuary, gilded again and behung with paintings and rows of closets that hold magnificent robes.

The sacristans, complicated bent old men, acting their parts like grand pensionaries of the Comédie Française, creep around in faded soutanes, carting silver candelabra, hanging up brocade curtains, arranging plants, and lighting or snuffing out candles—always followed by the large dark eyes of the Indians. Altar boys run around and chase one another except in front of the altar—they are Indian boys with black hair and brown, round faces over pink cassocks and white surplices. They finally line up at the door of the sacristy—one has an old and heavy silver censer which he begins to swing, another holds a set of small bells, and the one in the middle carries a tall, thin silver and gold cross. He has discovered that a ring of gold at the height

THE PLAZA INDEPENDENCIA, QUITO

of his nose, when touched with his tongue at the same time
as the silver, gives out a tingling sour taste, and so he licks
that part like a small dog during the procession and the
mass.

Bim-bim bim-bim, the bell up above begins. *Vamos*—
let's go—and they march into the church. The Protestant
religion, they told me, never made much progress here, because the pastors lack the power to forgive sins; but the
Catholic Church is busy all day long. One mass ends, another begins—there are litanies, sermons, adorations, ves-
pers, benedictions, novenas, forty-hour devotions, rosaries,
all day long. Bim-bim-bim. Bang-bang-bang.

Even the poorest sections of Quito have music and design. From the most decayed hovel leaning against its
neighbor comes the sound of a guitar, and the building is
made interesting by several coats of whitewash, each a different shade, as if three large bedsheets of varying degrees
of use, one above another, were draped over it. Other houses
insist on a character of their own by being painted with
the left-over colors of some better abode, coming out red,
blue, green, and mauve. People here are brave with colors,
and magnificent names are written over the doors of the
humblest houses.

The roofs are universally nice, bent, of tile so old that it
is green and gray, with small fields of light and blind,
smoky sides with the edges worn. The tiles are curved, two
rows with the concave side uppermost and between them
a third row, reversed, covering the joint. The evidence of
the hand and of play is everywhere; exactly the point where
someone grew tired of painting his house is visible in a final
upward stroke of the brush. There are peculiar designs

above windows and doors; benches are built into walls; chimneys lean and balconies sag.

The houses, good and poor, all have patios. In some of them are chickens and workbenches and in the others pools of water or a fountain, an arrangement of palms, cacti, and tangerine trees. You find floors done in colored tiles, inlaid with the vertebrae of oxen, walked on until the bone has taken on the feeling of old ivory, and so arranged that the inlay forms a design or spells the family name, the date of the house, the name of a favorite saint, or a motto.

Some of the patios are also painted with landscapes or naïve, bright designs done with great individuality, sometimes by the owner of the house. There are majolica vases with a thousand small cracks in them and banisters, doorways, columns, and cornucopias which show restraint, good judgment of space, and a quiet humor. It is all old, worn, bleached, and made by hand.

With these ancient, fine, and practical examples in front of you, it is doubly saddening to go into the modern quarter, into what is the elegant suburb, and see what they have done there. A pastrycook of an architect who has become fashionable has been let loose here and built a street in which he has carefully assembled everything that is bad and awful.

The first house is a Moroccan château, pink and green, with a memory of the Taj Mahal injected somewhere among its doors and windows. Next to it he has given shape to the nostalgia of a German émigré and perpetrated a Black Forest chalet that lacks only snow, Christmas music, pine trees, and a wolf with a basket in its mouth. The third exercise of his unhappy initiative is modern, a pastel-colored

bathroom turned inside out, a shiny small box with oversized round windows, oval doors, and a chromium ship's
rail on its roof. This row of houses, each one a few feet from
the other, ends in a stone sentinel, a midget Lohengrin
castle. Every one of these villas has been indulged with a
wall or fence, lanterns, doorknobs, bells, and landscaping
to match its character—the fixtures seem all personally
selected by the architect.

Happy to be out of this street, you run into another
architectural disaster a few blocks to the north—one that
is even more depressing because you cannot even laugh. In
a superb landscape that is difficult to equal, an ambitious
builder has set down two rows of houses facing each other—
about twenty of them, alike as foxterriers, built of stone,
painted red, with carefully drawn white lines dividing the
red surface into bricks. Each little house has the same number of windows, the same door, and the same mat of grass
to the left and right of the entrance. They accomplish the
heartlessness of a company street in the Pennsylvania coal
districts.

The owners of all these properties are extremely proud
of them, and one can console oneself by thinking of their
happiness and by riding away in any direction. In one
short hour from Quito, to the south, is a replica of the road
from Nice to Monte Carlo; to the west, Africa with bananas, Negroes, monkeys, and malaria; to the north, the
badlands of the Dakotas; to the east, Capuchin and Do-
minican monks in sandals, walking over soft carpets of
green grass like those along the Danube between Stift,
Melk, and Linz.

5.

About the Inhabitants of
Quito. On page 110 of a geography book that is
used in the schools of Ecuador, written by Professor Juan
Morales, the character of the natives of Quito is described
in detail.

I requested one of the pupils to translate the passage
into English and here is the paragraph verbatim:

"About the inhabitants of Quito: The character of his
[Quito's] inhabitants is laughing, frank and sincere, noble
and full of these qualities that are a gift and they are
learned. Is besides extremely patriot and lofty and incon-
taminated by any moral misery, but we must call attention
to a quality in this noble town that is called 'Sal Quiteña,'
is a quality that every Quiteño like to make joke of every
word they talk and like to smile with their funny word."

He forgot to say that they are also extremely generous,
polite, hospitable to a fault, and proud.

They certainly are patriots—no people on earth can
love their city more. They will take you by the arm and
hold you tight and whisper, "*Lindo, no?*—Is beautiful, no?
You love my country, yes?—Ah, you are so intelligent!"
And then they will say, "We Quiteños, when we die, we hope
to go to heaven, but we will go there only if we know that
in the floor there is an aperture, where we can kneel down
and look at our beautiful Quito."

The old Quito families stay in their homes and on their
haciendas. They love their children and the children love

their parents, deeply, genuinely; they care little for fashion.

The social life of Quito centers in and flows through the bar, the palm court, and the foyer of the Hotel Metropolitano and is mostly made up of foreigners.

Isaac J. Aboab, the energetic proprietor of this hotel, has assembled under its roof some hundred potted palms, uncomfortable beds, employees who are very obliging and run around all day with Flit guns, keeping the house free from flies and bugs. The kitchen is passable, there is always hot water, and an elevator runs day and night.

The palms stand in the palm court, their leaves gray and dead, the stems wound with old coco-matting. A row of splintered spreading wicker chairs, almost black with countless coats of varnish and sticky with a recent one, leans left or right of the palms between which they stand; they are upholstered in green velvet and decorated with a doily for your head to rest on. Next to each chair is again a brass spittoon, large enough to hold a bouquet of lilies. A landscape done by a native artist represents a waterfall along the Pastaza; the effect is very modern—like noodle soup running down over a green couch. At the door and between the chairs, in front of the elevator and on all the floors, are boys in caps with "Hotel Metropolitano" lettered in gold; they open and close doors, address the guests by name, jump here and there to catch a falling pocketbook, light cigars and cigarettes, and deliver messages. The service is excellent.

On Sunday afternoon, the solid bourgeois families, consisting of husband and wife and their two marriageable daughters, gather here to admire the scene and the people

of fashion and importance and to drink tea. The girls wear
wide-brimmed sailor hats and middy blouses, and hide their
long, black-stockinged legs from the glare of the Italian
Chargé d'Affaires. Quito, little town of churches, of tradi-
tion and above all of family ties, is jam-packed with lega-
tions and the cars that belong to them. The mail is shot
through with engraved invitations:

*"A l'occasion de la naissance du prince héritier, le minis-
tre de Bulgarie et Madame Popoff prient*, etc. etc." *"Der
deutsche Botschafter beehrt sich, Herrn und Frau—und so
weiter*." "The American Minister and Mrs. Longworth in-
vite all Americans to celebrate the Fourth of July."

Luncheons, dinners, dances, receptions, visits, and pres-
entations of credentials, the feasts of all the saints of the
Catholic Church and of several local Madonnas, the cele-
brations of the various independence days and great
battles, the birthdays of Sucre and Bolívar and the current President, keep Quito in a beflagged mood the year
round and cut schooldays down to 79 a year.

There are palace intrigues, counter-intrigues, fidelities
and infidelities among the foreign set, but among the Quiteños there seems to be some kind of regularity in family
affairs.

"Here in Quito," the father of a large and distinguished
family and a former President said sadly, "we have not to
offer the passing, loose pleasures of the big city. Here in
Quito, Señor, either you love your wife or you go to visit
New York, or if you are very fortunate to Paris; but, alas,
Paris and New York are so far away, the exchange is so bad
just now . . . next year, perhaps, when the Germans can
buy our coffee and chocolate again, we can go to Paris."

A lieutenant was even more gloomy. A careless sun-burned man, his eyes covered by dark lids and lashes, he looked down at the table, slowly unpacked a box of matches and put them back one by one, and sighed:

"It is terrible here, Señor. First you must make love to this girl you want until your nose bleeds; second you must make love not only to her but to her mother, her father, the butler, and the parrot, and in the end you always must marry her."

"Always?" I said.

"Always," he assured me bleakly. "The town is too small —for otherwise, with a desirable girl"—he put up his hands and counted the obstacles—"she is religious, that is one fence you must jump over; she is beautiful; she is rich, that is the third fence—but the worst is that the streets and the windows are full of relatives who watch her. There are three Pizarro aunts, three Ayora aunts, two Chirimoya uncles, and a Rio del Pinar family of twelve head, and her father—he is worse than all of them. He had the cheek to ask the British Minister for a list of his guests before he accepted for her—what do you think of that?"

Outside of the marriage market, things are not too difficult, at least as far as boys are concerned.

"My wife is a modern woman," said another family man. "She reads American magazines, she has a subscription to the *Woman's Home Companion*, and they are full of these things, I mean about certain big diseases, and she is afraid that our boy Anselmo will get it, too.

" 'Do you know,' she says in the middle of the night, 'that ninety percent in this country have it, and the other ten are getting it?' She is like a dictator when she says these things. 'We must know,' she said, 'with whom he goes, or else he will run around and ruin himself. Look at your cousin Alfonso,' she said; 'he is sick and he has difficulty in walking; they say that it is rheumatism but it is that sickness. Good, it will not happen with our Anselmo.'

"Anselmo at the time was nineteen years old and a quiet boy; he was not sick, he was not fat, his voice had changed, but nothing happened. At one time at least we thought that something had happened with Clemencia the maid, a very quiet girl; but no. What will we do?

"All at once my wife thought of my brother who lives in Guayaquil, where these things are arranged more easily than in Quito. My brother is a man of the world, and he found a nice girl, very agreeable and serious, and he rented a small apartment and arranged a party. My brother first took Anselmo for a long drive and told him all about love and how things are between two people, and then he took him to the little place. The girl was properly presented to Anselmo and the arrangement seemed prudent; it lasted several weeks, until Anselmo got homesick and came back. The girl cried a little but made no demands, and my brother sent her a gift and flowers and Anselmo did not get the big illness, only the little one.

"And all this began with Mother, who was afraid of syphilis. 'I hope you are content now,' I have said to her."

Entertaining, among the elect families whose names are cut into marble plaques on the side of the cathedral, is difficult in Quito on account of the fact that all of them are related to one another, and when someone dies half the city is in mourning for six months. By the time they discard their black clothes, someone else is dead.

The more worldly families and the diplomats entertain mostly in their homes. With the few exceptions of French and Belgian hostesses, who trouble themselves with their kitchens, the dinners are starchy sessions of course after course which leave their traces in soft round arms, matronly profiles, padded wrists and fingers.

A clique of some hundred people forms the café society of Quito. Twice a day they repair to the bar of the Metropolitano; on Wednesday evenings they attend the gala performance at the Cinema Bolívar. You meet them on Sunday at the arena watching bullfights, and far into the night they sit at the tables of the nightclub that is currently in vogue. Here they repeat the meager gossip of the town and stare at newcomers with an insolence that is unmatched even in Berlin and Budapest restaurants—they all but come over to your table to read the labels on your clothes.

Of all the women here, perhaps half a dozen are beautiful and four of these dress with taste.

The last and most interesting group is a small circle of ever-changing characters, a formidable array of talents and personalities, who immediately recognize one another, link arms, and sit down together.

They are explorers, English remittance men, ex-Captains of the Foreign Legion, Hollywood stunt men, deep-sea divers, and promoters of various imaginative enterprises. Each one of them has a biography, brief and risky and as if clipped out of a magazine, and the man is usually a good illustration for the article.

Among this group was a pretender to the throne of Austria, for Quito, like every other metropolis, has its own outcropping of the Affaire Mayerling. Franz Josef's local grandson had some claim to authenticity: his accent was correct, he clicked his heels in the real sloppy Viennese fashion, he was heavy-lipped, and appeared always to be unhappy. At a reception, when he came to the buffet to get some hors d'œuvre for the girls out in the patio, he burdened his arms all the way up, past the elbow, with plates filled with food, stuck a bunch of forks inside his cummerbund, and whisked a napkin under his arm with the technique, if not of a Habsburg, at least of a grandson of that other old Franz Josef, the one at the Bristol in Vienna.

Next to him at the explorers' table usually sat Captain Cyril Vigoroux, a stout man with a beard and a tropical helmet, a hat which is frowned upon in Quito. ("This is not Africa," the natives say.) Doctor Cyril Vigoroux was at one time a ship's surgeon on an obscure vessel, a small ship known as the suicide boat. In the middle of the ocean, a woman squeezed herself out of a porthole and was gone. . . . A few latitudes farther on, after Neptune had come aboard as they passed the Equator, they found among the débris and the pieces of decoration and costumes that had come off during the celebration, at the bottom of the canvas pool, the body of a Rhodes scholar . . . and the next day an old lady was taken ill, Doctor Cyril Vigoroux diagnosed acute appendicitis, had the steamer stopped and operated on her, and to the surprise of the old lady, the ship, and even the doctor, she lived, came up on deck awhile later, and walked off the boat in New York. Years later she died and left all her money to the doctor. He exchanged the anonymity of a ship's surgeon for a membership in the Explorers' Club and the fame and glory that goes with voyaging to places where no one has been before.

The third man at the table was a silent man, a man in whose face were several animals: an Irish setter, a thoroughbred, affectionate horse—and around the nose up near the bridge a good deal of character. His forehead was usually corrugated with worry. He was an explorer who had come to seek gold, the only dependable-looking man at the table. He sat in profound silence, smoked a pipe and allowed his beard to grow, asked a few questions about terrain and weather, and occasionally changed the way his legs were crossed. He looked at the ceiling, out into the street, then a long while at the waiter, and when the waiter looked at him, he raised his eyebrows and so did the waiter, and brought him another gin and tonic. Ferguson was his name, Allan Ferguson; he seemed to be an honest man and really wanted to look for gold.

During one of the great silences of Allan Ferguson I looked with him out into the street. A woman passed, an Indian, barefoot, with twelve boards of wood strapped to her back. The boards reached in a diagonal line from a few inches above the street to perhaps three feet beyond her head: she moved quickly in a trot and uphill, quieting the baby which was suspended from her in a piece of cloth.

A beggar also passed—a statue of misery, in a well-thought-out costume—in an overcoat that was as old as the man, made of small patches of cloth, each one the size of a matchbox, a garment that forever renewed itself. He had hard dry feet, a cane, a white beard, and like all the other beggars sold lottery tickets and sang, "*Veinte mil sucres.*" After he had passed the window, with a little black woman in black in front of him and a padre behind, a Rolls-Royce came along.

It was one of the used cars that one can buy for about a hundred dollars in New York. Gray and with a miniature tree of levers and throttles above its steering wheel, it had trouble turning corners, and filled the street from sidewalk to sidewalk. It was driven by a native chauffeur in a reversible leather coat. The radiator was covered with club emblems and its backside displayed "G.B." in thick letters on a square metal shield.

Ferguson remained silent, but Gerard de Kongaga, Minister of the Armenian Legation, who also sat at the explorers' table, leaned over and asked me whether I knew the owner of the car. "Thinks nothing of wearing suits like this"—Kongaga pulled his necktie out of his coat and showed its loud pattern—"hunting and fishing chap, lives right next to you"—I was staying in a small villa in the Mariscal section then—"fellow who owns that car."

"Englishman?" I asked.

"Ra-ther," said Kongaga, "remittance man, wonderful chap; here he comes."

6

The Morale of the Natives.

He appeared before me every morning, across a three-foot garden wall, somewhere between an acacia tree in full bloom and some lotuses that grew close to his balcony. He was nude at about nine in the morning and a small monkey sat on his fist; he sang, and then lay down on a couch to take a sunbath.

A little black boy in a white coat brought him his breakfast, rubbed him with some lotion, and then stood by to chase the flies away. At ten he went into his house and then appeared after short interludes, first in his underwear, next stuffing his shirt into his trousers, and eventually fully dressed. He tied his cravat in the sun; his song had no melody, it was a formless tra-la-laa, a noise made of the pleasure of living, completely thoughtless, without beginning or end. For the rest of the day, when he was home, Captain Alastair Monibuy shouted at his servants, played with his animals, and took pictures with a Leica—pictures of anything and anybody.

He had arrived in Quito in the old Rolls-Royce, making the perilous journey from Babahoyo, driving himself, a high testimonial to the motor and the chassis of the old car.

In the back of the car he had stowed several Louis Vuitton suitcases and a dozen polo mallets, a rifle and fishing gear, a saddle and a case of gin—gin was his favorite drink. His eyes were like two round emeralds, and when he drank they shone with hypnotic brilliance. He stood always tense, one leg a little ahead of the other, the upper body erect, shoulders back, one hand in his trouser pocket, playing with keys or change, and the other holding the glass tightly.

The whole little man was closely packed into good clothes, so tight that one felt the buttons on his suit or shirt would pop off any minute.

He first lived at the Metropolitano, but later found a little villa in the Mariscal section of Quito, an inexpensive livable house with a large garden and a garage, and a place where he could keep his zoo. He had a monkey and two tigrillos. (A tigrillo is really an ocelot, but having no tigers of their own, the Ecuadorians have elevated that animal to the rank of tiger, using the diminutive.) He had also a macaw and two parrots. His ménage was sloppy, as was his person. There was a drawer full of bottles of Geneva gin in the living room; cigarette butts and matches accumulated in the washbasins of all the rooms, and somewhere there was always a stack of empty bottles. Broken glasses in the fireplace, and a long blond hair or dandruff on his coat. His hair was sticky and dirty.

He had trained an Indian boy as a servant, a very attractive mulatto as a cook, and the mulatto's twelve-year-old daughter to make the beds and clean the house. He smacked them all across the backside with his riding crop whenever they passed by him, and then laughed a hearty ha-ha-ha-ha-ha, a furious signal that also escaped him after every short, loud, and deliberate sentence. He did not speak, he telegraphed his ideas and observations, leaving out all unnecessary words—the telegram always came in faultless English. He had been to Sandhurst, he said.

After he had asked me for lunch one day, he showed me how he had decorated his house. Nailed on the wall in the

living room hung a uniform in which he had flown for
Franco, and next to it was a large frame in which, behind
a glass, he had arranged an assortment of letterheads, with
most distinguished addresses printed on them. There were
about thirty of them and the best were: The Château de
Gande, The Athenaeum, Chequers, Ten Downing Street,
The Horse Guards, etc.

Each of these letters started with "Dear Bimbo," as he
was known to his intimates; but the text in every case save
one was hidden by the letter next to it. In the center of all
these expensive papers, in cream and oyster hues, was a
note from Hilaire Belloc, with text and signature showing,
acknowledging the gift of a book. Once, when he added a
new letter and had the whole correspondence laid out on the
table, in order to arrange it anew, some of the other letters
were laid bare. The one from the Athenaeum requested the
return of a loan; two others were regrets.

On the opposite wall hung another frame, into which he
had written "My Passions," and this contained photographs: a string of polo ponies, a Savoia-Marchetti sea-
plane, a yacht and a sailboat and several girls, all British
and pretty and blond, with their hair loose on top of their
heads; every one of them had signed herself "With love
to Bimbo."

He knew everybody and he had several kinds of behavior
and fitted himself into almost any group. He never said
anything, but his loud ha-ha-ha-ha followed every word he
said and was infectious. People laughed and did not know
why. He was the only completely happy man I have ever
known; he lacked the capacity to worry.

Bimbo rode well, was a generous host, made compliments

to the old ladies, and hopped from table to table. The doors of all good houses were open to him; he had, when he was in need of them, passable manners, and he had so ingratiated himself that he was permitted to come late everywhere and even sit down to dinner in riding clothes and mud-caked boots. Many a father thought that at last a man worthy of his beautiful but still unmarried daughter had arrived in Quito; dressmakers worked, florists were busier, wine merchants, butchers, and even saddlemakers felt the presence of Captain Alastair Monibuy.

One day he gave a cocktail party at his villa. He stood at the entrance playing with the change in his trouser pocket, pounding guests on the shoulder as they arrived, and roaring cheer.

The villa was filled, every room loud with conversation, long past the time when people usually went home. A dinner was hastily put together, some extra drinks made. It lasted late into the night. When almost everyone had finally departed, there was a scream from above, and then a body fell down the stairs.

It was the Armenian Minister, Gerard de Kongaga. This diplomat of good family and most amiable disposition had clamped himself to the banister, after talking to himself in the corner of the corridor above for half an hour, and then he had let go.

Kongaga had spent most of his life in Schönbrunn in one of the famous retreats of Professor Lorand, a healer who believed in occupational therapy. Kongaga had built so much garden furniture and so many birdhouses that he had become an expert carpenter and painter.

Since his arrival in Ecuador, however, he had never been

sober. When he came to parties it was in the manner of a
blind man who has lost his dog: he saw people where none
stood, and offered them his hand in greeting. That day, as
he came up the stairs, he passed the host, mistook the Papal
Nuncio for the French Minister, embraced him, and told
him dirty stories. He recognized the host later on and went
up to him, held on to Monibuy to steady himself for a while,
and then turned and looked into the room full of people.
One could see him calculate his moves; he narrowed his eyes
and surveyed his chances. There was a table filled with
glasses to the right; a few feet away, opposite that hazard,
stood a statue on a taboret, and beyond this was a chair
with a lady in it, the British Minister's wife. Wanting to
say something nice to that lady, and observing that next
to her was a vacant chair, he decided to sit down. He smiled
at the Papal Nuncio, let go of Monibuy's hand, stood
straight up, buttoned his coat, and then—one, two, three,
—he started off. . . . The lady was not there; it was a tall
vacant Jacobean chair, upholstered, that had looked occupied. The chair next to it was there, so he took the arm
rests into his hands and, with the dolorous mechanism of a
paralytic, sat down—between the two chairs—pulling both
down over him. He was rescued with great effort and seated
in the chair on the left, and then he was quiet until the
people who had lifted him up turned away and began to
talk again. Then he plotted again and thought up a new
and perfected excursion—which ended up in the fireplace.

He never became violent, his gentle face expressed nothing but a mild disappointment; he liked everyone and
everyone liked Gerard de Kongaga. The women openly regretted that the rich, good-looking, and gallant man had

few sober moments. He fell loosely like an acrobat and seldom came to grief. At Monibuy's cocktail party he had fallen well again, and the host, the mulatto cook, and the Habsburg dragged him upstairs to the guest room and covered him up.

When the party finally began to break up, Bimbo decided that he could not sleep and wanted to go to the Ermitage, the El Morocco of Quito. The Ermitage was located in an old house. The policeman on duty in the street outside, the Carabinero Number 18, made himself useful opening and closing automobile doors, smiling at people, and acting as the doorman. In his faded greatcoat with the big saber at his side, he had gone better with the place when it was called Volga Volga. Like all the policemen in Quito, he was a half-breed. He had an old handkerchief tied around his face to protect nose and throat from the cold; but he kept this in his pocket on mild evenings and amused himself by imitating the songs of various birds, for he was an accomplished whistler. The rooms of the Ermitage were low and dim and so badly upholstered that when a patron sat down on one of the imitation leopard-skin banquettes, the patrons who sat to his left and right bounced up and down several inches. Cheap glass and crockery were on its tables, badly painted Russian murals with troikas and snow and the cathedral of Kazan painted on the walls, left over from the days when the place was under White Russian management. From that period also remained a large glass globe which showered the room with snow effects when the lights were turned low. The place was managed by two Frenchwomen, Lydia and Tamara, each with a friend in the Government and excellent business acumen. One smoked from a long cigarette holder; the other sat on a high stool, and twice an evening she played a guitar and sang such ballads as "*Ma femme est morte.*" Champagne was compulsory, the prices were out of reason, the music was native, and when they tried to play such things as "St. Louis Blues" or "South of the Border," two of their favorites, it took awhile to recognize the tune; and then the flutes pulled your scalp tight and made your ears wiggle. But late at night, when they played their own music, their native music which is in somewhat the same beat as a two-step, they played with fine rhythm. The *crème de la crème* of Quito assembled here; it was particularly crowded on Fridays, the shoddy linoleum dance-floor half set with chairs and tables.

At midnight on the day of the cocktail party, when Bimbo and the Habsburg were driving to the Ermitage, after taking off a door of the car coming out of the gate of the villa, they heard a voice from the back seat. It was Gerard de Kongaga and he said, "You fellows aren't mad at me, I hope." They stopped the car and told him that they were not mad at him, that they were very happy he had come along. The old Rolls-Royce squeezed itself through the streets of Quito with its loud special horn going tatitata all the way to the Ermitage.

Kongaga crawled out of the car into the arms of his friends, and the three of them entered the room and advanced to the bright light where Tamara had just finished singing a couplet. Everyone became wide-eyed, Lydia quickly rushed to dim the room and turned on the snow effect, and the ladies looked the other way. Gerard de Kongaga stood in the center of the dance-floor minus his trousers. The room was darkened, the music started, and a waiter ran out for the policeman-doorman.

When the Carabinero Number 18 came in, he laughed and tried to be very friendly. He stood in front of Kongaga and tried to hide him from the audience with his big coat. Kongaga was busy twisting at the only button which was left on the policeman's coat; little pieces of thread hung empty where the others had been and the coat was held together by the belt from which the saber was suspended. The policeman tried to make himself part of the fun and hooked his arm into Kongaga's and said, "*Vamos!* Come on, let's go! Let's go home—no?" and started to pull him slowly from the room. This did not go well with Captain Monibuy. He looked hard at the policeman and then tore him away from Kongaga. "Take your hands off that man instantly— let go now! Do you know who that is? That is His Excellency the Armenian Minister"—but the little policeman said again, "*Vamos*—let's go home," and pulled on Kongaga's sleeve once more. Monibuy drew his shoulder back and hit the policeman so hard that he fell, spun, and disappeared—all but his small feet—under a ringside table. There was quiet again and the Habsburg dragged Kongaga out to the Rolls-Royce and they drove him home.

The next day Monibuy was in his little summerhouse in the garden. He came out in a bathrobe, and he shouted over the wall, "You know, I wore out a suit last night; they ripped the sleeves out of my dinner coat." His boy brought a bloater and he drank some tea. He sat in the morning sun for a while and his boy rubbed him down. At about eleven a car drove up, a policeman appeared and announced that the Chief of Police was in the car, and asked whether he might come in. The Chief came and put his cap and saber away, took off his gloves, and had some tea. He leaned back in his seat and looked up at Pichincha and over at Cayambe and said, "What a lovely day. It was . . . you love my country? Ah, I am glad, is beautiful, no? And such lovely weather." He changed his tone and kept his hands busy snapping his gloves together and taking them apart again. Then he watched the labor of some ants on the garden wall and said wearily, "I am a very busy man, I am perhaps too serious. So many things happen, stupid things, and everybody comes to me with their troubles. I think there was some trouble last night—I do not go out much, I do not know much of these places—I hear in a place called the Ermitage, and somebody—I have not heard the name— I think with perhaps a little too much to drink, comes there, without proper dress . . . and there is a fight. Nothing important—it happens all the time, it happens everywhere —but I wish people would not hit our policemen; it is so bad for the morale of the natives."

7

The Boots of General Altamir Pereira.

I had lost a pair of English boots by leaving them too close to a campfire in Patagonia. I woke up the next morning and the soles fell off them, the soft part over the ankles was like lint, and I held the shafts in my hand. They were costly and very old, they had been on many rides, and ever since I had lost them I was sad whenever I thought of them, the shop where they were made, and the fine color they had turned.

I saw a pair of well-cut boots hanging out of a fauteuil in the lobby of the Club Pichincha one afternoon, and I asked my friend Manuel Pallares to tell me whom they belonged to. Manuel immediately introduced me to the man who wore them, General Altamir Acyr Pereira.

You must never admire anything too much in this hospitable land, because it becomes the immediate duty of most people to make you a present of it. The General regretted that he could not take off his boots there and then and give them to me, but he promised that the next day his personal bootmaker, one Leopoldo Sandoval, would present himself at my residence and bring with him a hide, a selected hide from the prize cattle of the General's own hacienda in Antisana. The bootmaker would then take my measure for a pair of boots exactly like the General's own.

He asked me what hour would be convenient, and then clapped his hands for the mayordomo of the Club Pichincha. This man came, stood at attention with his fingers glued to the seams of his trousers, and repeated to the Gen-

eral word for word that tomorrow at ten Leopoldo Sandoval would come to me with the hide of the prize cattle of
Antisana and make me a pair of boots with the compliments
of the General. He turned and gave this order to another
servant, who took a cap and ran.

I sat in stocking feet in the patio of the house the next
morning and waited. Monibuy dressed and sang. A man
with a beard and golden spectacles came and wanted to sell
me an interest in some caves that were filled with bat ma-
nure, a most wonderful fertilizer. And finally Kongaga
came and said, "Don't tell me you are waiting for the cobbler, that you believe you will get those boots! Talk, talk,
beautiful talk, that's all it is. They sing these things off like
the national anthem. 'My house, my horses, my hacienda
are yours.' But it doesn't mean a thing."

The cobbler was late, but he came. Leopoldo Sandoval
appeared with the hide and a boy and a piece of brown
paper. In the garden house he put my feet on the paper
one after the other and drew around them with a pencil,
taking measurements and dictating all the details to his
son. He snapped out the numbers and retired backward
out of the house, to turn around only when he was twenty
feet away, after making a last compliment and bow, together with the small son.

The boots, comfortable and elegant, arrived a few days
after a fitting, and with them an invitation from the General to visit him. He lived in a palace in the center of Quito,
in a cool old Spanish baroque house, with a garden large
enough to race horses in. The rooms in his house were on
two floors, the apartments large enough to entertain two
or three hundred people.

At the door was a heavy crocheted portiere whose lowest fringe struck me just under the nose. Bending under this, you entered the room. Four fountains made of marble stood on the edges of a flowered red carpet in an inner sanctum determined by a quadrangle of mother-of-pearl columns. In each of the fountains were two silver birds of paradise, one with his head down, the other up.

In the exact center of this carpet stood a circular sofa, such a one as stands in the first-class waiting room of the railroad station at Monte Carlo. People sit in a ring around it, legs outside, backs together, and over them is a jardiniere with ferns and a palm.

Between three high and wide windows, framed in heavy green velvet portieres with hundreds of pompons, stood Louis Seize chairs, authentic pieces. Hanging between the windows in large frames were sepia-tinted photographs of the Flatiron Building, the Roman Colosseum, and the Hotel Plaza in New York. The General told me he loved America.

One wall was dominated by a family group, the General and Doña Faviola, and around them their nine sons, reading from left to right: Alejandro–Aquilino–Alfonso–Arquimedes–Antonio–Arturo–Altamir–Anselmo–Antenor.

The space on the other wall was taken up almost entirely by a large painting, a Swiss landscape. It was not only high and wide, but also thick. The General took a key from a vitrine, and found a small keyhole in a door that was painted on a house in an Alpine village in the lower left corner of the picture. He inserted the key and turned it and music began to play. The painting became alive: a small train chuffed out of a tunnel and ran over a bridge, a Montgolfier balloon rose in the air, descended and went

up again, and two blacksmiths hammered on an anvil. I
was afraid to admire the picture too much, because the hospitable General might have given it to me. The music
slowed, the train also, and the Montgolfier bag sank in its
last descent as we sat down to eat.

The General said that he had heard that I wanted to go
into the jungles of Oriente and up to the headwaters of the
Amazon. He had a large hacienda in the jungle, he said,
and three of his sons were in there, Altamir, Arquimedes,
and Anselmo, very lonesome and happy to see anybody.

The way in started from Baños, and to Baños he would
send me in a car. I would have to stay there awhile, and
from there a truck would take me to the Río Negro, and
then horses on into the jungle.

"My home, my servants, my horses are at your command
—and I think you had better take a boy along to look after
you."

He clapped his hands again and his mayordomo arrived.
He asked him to call a boy named Aurelio.

"This is the boy you need. He usually rides with me. He
speaks a little English. He will take care of you." The boy
came and the General said to him, "Go with this man, he is
your *patrón*," and to me, "Send him back when you are
through with him."

Aurelio from then on was never more than six feet from
me. Even in the dark, when I had completely forgotten that
he was there, he stood silently in back of me. He always
smiled, he never was tired, he picked things off the floor and
chairs and hung them up. He had the curiosity of a young
dog and he warmed the lonesomeness of the long rides with

his simple English phrases. The first one he tried out on me
was, "I love you, Mother."

He ran along to help me pack my things. Just then two
planes roared over the Metropolitano. He went to the window and looked up, and then he said to me in Spanish, "One
day they will come over, hundreds of them, and kill us all
with them, with these machines, with bombs that come down."

"Who," I said, "will come and do that?"

"Oh, the damned Yanquis."

"And who told you that?"

"Oh, everybody knows that."

"But who told you?"

"Ah, it's real knowledge," he said. "My brother, who can
read, has found this written many times in the magazine
called *The Voice of the Worker*. My brother drives a bus,
and he gets fifteen sucres a week for calling the bus 'Adolfo
Hitler,' because it's a nice new bus. And other bus drivers
get ten sucres for calling the bus 'Hindenburg' or 'Ale-
mania' or 'Berlino' or 'Hamburgo' or 'Zeppelin.' The busses
go through the city and to the villages. 'Adolfo Hitler' runs
from here to Machachi."

We passed "Adolfo Hitler" on the road the next day.
Aurelio waved to his brother, and in three hours' ride we
came to the Pension Hilda in Ambato, again, like most
pensions, run by Germans.

On the stretch between Pelileo and Baños we found a
bus called "Zeppelin" with a broken wheel, its forty passengers standing around it. Farther on there was rain and
a landslide. We had to climb over it and found "Napoleon
I" waiting there. In this vehicle we rode on to Baños.

Near the old empty stone church in Baños, whose walls are shrill with the mettlesome complaints of sparrows, is a holy pool of copper-colored hot water. A stream of the heavy fluid breaks through the rock out of the side of a mountain. Cooling off in wooden gutters, it runs down into the pool in two streams, each one the thickness of a strong man's arm. It runs from a stone urn, then thins out, becomes a few shades lighter, and falls heavily into the waters below. There are no bubbles. Outside of a gulping sound there is no disturbance. It is like hot sirup, hard to wade and swim in.

The water is let out every night and two Indians scrape the residue, a golden slime, from the walls of the stone pool. They go to an icy waterfall that comes down the mountain ten feet to the left of the pool, get buckets of water, and throw them into the eight dressing rooms that the community of Baños has erected for the convenience of visitors.

That is the only thing they have done, cut the stones for the pool, built the cabins, and appointed the Indians to keep it clean at night. All else has been left undisturbed—there is no sign, no list of rules, no one to rent out bathing suits, and no tickets needed. Early in the morning or late in the afternoon you can go there and be alone, and it is as if you found the pool in a far-away field.

At the edge of the pool sheep and cattle graze, their hoofs buried in Alpine plants and small flowers. The land descends in terraces to the church, to another pool that is filled with dark brown, icy mineral water, and to the far emerald-green fields of sugar cane that fill the valley like a wide river.

All around soar mountains so steep, so rigid that the
light seems to tumble over them. The mountains remain
opaque as if dark green chalk were rubbed over a rough
black paper. After you look at them for a long time the
shapes of trees and plants appear, softly and loosely
sketched.

In the early morning, in the first daylight, when the sun
rises high up near the glaciers, clouds like the bellies of a
thousand whales crowd themselves down over the valley.
The sun shines above them, and some light comes through.
Then everything swims in bluish milk; veils of gray gauze
fall over trees and houses and change all the distances.
They stay awhile, lift again, sometimes dissolve, and when
they come down too close, the air currents over the wild
waters of the Pastaza tug on their edges, tear them up,
stretch them out, and drag them down toward the jungle.

People come to the holy waters of Baños with twisted
hands and with rheumatic troubles, and some of them can
hardly walk when they arrive. The water is indeed miracu-
lous. It cures most of them, and the few that are not cured
are better when they go than they were.

What is gained in the baths is undone in the hotels and
pensions of Baños. Fortunately there are few, and all of
them are small. The beds are damp, sagging, narrow cots,
the legs unsteady. The food is abominable in all. I took a
room in the most highly recommended and most comfortable of these places, the Gran Hotel Astor. It stood in front
of an untidy yard facing the pool, looking as if a small
child had designed it—a window in the center of the upper
floor, and one, two, three irregular windows more to the
left and right; a door under the center window and six

more windows below; a roof, a chimney, some smoke, and, over the door, "Gran Hotel Astor" written in crude letters. In every one of its windows, instead of a curtain, hang the wet bathing suit and towel of a guest. Over the door is the date when this sorry edifice was finished. There is the screaming of children, and no one comes to receive you. In the lobby is a poster in Spanish: "Come to Germany, the land of music and culture."

Going through the house I found in one of the rooms a young Indian woman, barefoot, singing with a broom in her hand. She was the entire staff. She waited for me to speak. She then thought for a few seconds about whether a room was vacant. Ecuador is the paradise of hoteliers. No matter how bad, their hotels are always filled. She remembered after a while and after having looked at it that there was a room, but she said we must first go down and see the proprietress.

This woman is usually to be found in the doorway between the kitchen and the dining room, and she is German also. She frowns into the kitchen from habit, then turns and smiles into the dining room, because a guest is usually there.

She fell into a few pleasantries that day, and looking at the Indian, she said, *"Oh, diese Naturkinder,"* and explained that the girl, whose name was Luz María, "the Mary of Light," was fond of animals, and that she had discovered that she kept a nest of small birds in a silver drawer in the dining room. The silver Madame referred to was an assortment of greasy knives and battered spoons, and forks with half their prongs bent or missing.

"This way," said the woman, and I walked out of the

kitchen and around the edge of a loamy yard, red with water that ran off between the stones of the pool.

The room was on the second floor, close to a bath. The bath had a long narrow tub, and a tall stove was attached to it. The bed was still unmade, the doorhandle came off as the door was shut, and the only good thing about any of the thirty-five rooms of this hotel was the view from their windows. The Gran Hotel Astor is on a most enviable site, overlooking the pool and the village. Aurelio slept on the floor at the foot of my bed, and we waited for the mayordomo of the Hacienda El Triunfo to come with his truck and take us in toward the jungle.

8

Benitin and Eneas. In this village,

in Baños, is a small restaurant called the American Country
Club. It used to be run by two men who were partners in
this enterprise, one named Benitin and the other Eneas.

Benitin and Eneas are the Spanish names of Mutt and
Jeff in the American comic strip which appears in trans-
lation in the newspaper *El Comercio* in Quito. The res-
taurateurs were known by these names because one was
tall, the other short, and also because their real names—
they signed themselves Vorkapitch and Sasslavsky on all
official documents—were too difficult for the Castilian ears
of their clientele.

The general equipment of a restaurant in this land demands no great amount of capital. The local painter makes
a sign for it, and you need in addition a strong padlock for
the door, four tables, twelve chairs, a few glasses and plates
new or old, tinware and a corkscrew and two salt and pepper shakers and a bottle of imitation Worcestershire sauce
—and the dining room is taken care of. At the bar is a box
for the ice which the Indians bring down from the glaciers,
a kind of hard, sooty snow, and the light comes from one
weak bulb, without a shade, that hangs on a wire in the
precise center of the room together with a sheet of flypaper.
The flypaper acts as a sail, so that whenever the door is
opened the light is carried to the left or right, and in a busy
restaurant, in consequence of this, the shadows of every
object are constantly in motion.

There is some kind of oven in the room and a pan to
wash dishes. To divide kitchen from restaurant a curtain

is hung, and with two pots and pans, the kitchen is ready.

What lifted the American Country Club into the rank of a *restaurant de grand luxe*, however, was that Benitin had invested in a music machine—a highly polished smooth cabinet with a slot into which a sucre could be dropped. When this happened, the instrument began to hum for a while, lit itself up in brilliant rainbow hues, and then rendered six pieces of staccato music to which people danced, while the Indians sat at a respectful distance outside the club and listened until the doors were closed.

Eneas, the other partner, had come through with an equally elegant contribution: he had installed two water-closets, one for caballeros and the other for señoras. The advertisements of the American Country Club featured both "dancing" and "confort moderne."

The room was small and usually crowded, and warm. The ceiling was low. Benitin and his music machine were out in front. He attended to the four tables there and kept watch over the two dozen bottles of assorted spirits which comprised the cellar of the club.

Eneas and his investment were in back of the curtain. He crouched over a low inadequate oven, cooked, made ham and chicken and club sandwiches, and talked to himself.

Eneas was not satisfied. The place was the only restaurant in Baños, it was in an excellent position facing the plaza, and it did good business for luncheon, dinner, and late into the night. He stood behind the curtain all day long until closing time; he did most of the work while the other one hung over the bar out front, laughed and talked with the customers, poured himself drinks, and listened to the music.

"Why," said Eneas to himself, and to anyone who came behind and listened to him, "why should I work like a dog and split the profits with him? This town can stand another restaurant."

The next time he found himself in bad humor, he took advantage of a routine dispute with his partner and declared in his native Czech that he was through being a poodle, that he wanted his share of the business and also the watercloset.

A watercloset in this remote valley is a rare convenience. It is not only a testimonial to the initiative of its owner; it costs a good deal of money. Once ordered, its arrival is problematic; landslides will delay it, bridges may be washed away, there is the chance of breakage or of total loss. The time that passes between the day it is ordered and that when a donkey finally brings it to the door is one of chagrin and suspense.

It is easy to understand why Eneas insisted on taking his investment with him to his new restaurant. The new place, which was immediately next door, was higher; it had once been a Government building, sported two Ionic columns and a coat of arms over its door. It had fallen into neglect, but Eneas had painters busy for a week, put a carpet on the floor, built a solid division between dining room and kitchen, and hired an artist from Ambato to decorate the interior.

At the entrance next to the columns he placed two large palms, and from the ceiling he hung Japanese paper lanterns with red 75-watt bulbs in them. He even entertained the idea of having an electric sign made with "Salon Hollywood" flashing on and off.

After the "confort moderne" was properly installed to the left and right, Eneas hired a native cook and he himself put on a chef's hat and supervised the preparation of the specialties of the house.

His tables, in accusing contrast to the American Country Club, were covered with clean checkered tablecloths. For most of the day Eneas now stood out in front waiting for his guests, his new waiters in a semi-circle around him, alert as pointing dogs.

It was all in vain.

Next door, without even whitewash on its walls, the American Country Club was crowded; people laughed and danced to the music of Xavier Cugat and Enrique Madriguera, corks were pulled and glasses broken, the noise went on until dawn. But Eneas continued to stand alone among his empty tables and chairs. At long-spaced intervals a hurried customer came running from next door, ordered a drink, and asked Eneas to turn on the light in the back, but the rest of the time his place yawned with emptiness and failure.

A month after he had opened it, Eneas closed the Salon Hollywood. The chairs and tables he sold to Benitin. The confort moderne he decided to take with him.

Four donkeys inside the Salon Hollywood stood loaded with the heavy porcelain, the fixtures, pipes, and water tanks. Eneas gave his last instructions to the Indian who was to deliver the cargo in Ambato, and then he sat down under a striped new awning on one of his own chairs, in

the midst of his tables and palms, which now were all part
of a sidewalk café in front of the American Country Club.
His former partner Benitin served him some rice and mutton. Eneas took a half-hearted bite and then pushed the
plate away and stared out into the plaza.

This square is formed by three rows of houses half fallen
apart, maroon, yellow, green, and black. Two have no roofs
and moss grows on the tiles of the others. The doors, the
balconies, the stones at the entrances have all been shifted
to conflicting angles by earthquakes, and there is one balcony that makes the heart stop beating. It is high up and
has no railing, just three short beams coming out of the
house with two pieces of rotted gray board laid over them;
and out on this platform a baby crawls every day to play
and listen to the music of the American Country Club.

A few feet north of the center of the square stands an
immense, fanciful tree. Its wide branches carry stout green
leaves the shape and color of laurel. The trunk of the tree
is bent and twisted and it is as if it were hammered out of
dull silver. Most of the leaves hang down over a fountain,
a severe octagonal basin which, like all the stone in this
humid valley, is soft and enchanting under a coverlet of
fan-shaped miniature greenery. At the side where the water
spills over the stone hang long beards of dripping grass,
and from this grass the water flows down across the wide
steps that encircle the fountain. The water quietly enters
a large puddle that is in the exact center of the square. In
this dark brown water a white church reflects itself, making
the fourth side of the square. On days when the sun shines,
shadows heavy and black, like blankets of indigo, lie under
the tree; the water in the fountain is black and the only

light comes from a basket full of lemons spread in front of
an Indian woman sitting under the tree, and from the ponchos of besotted customers over in the native tienda across
the square.

Into this scene Eneas looked for the last time. His donkeys, loaded with the confort moderne, passed the tree and
their gray hides were reflected in the puddle. They drank
from the fountain and one of them raised his head, showed
his teeth, and began his peculiar song. The church bell
clanked and a sudden wind shifted the spray of the fountain. More water spilled and ran down over the side.

The Salon Hollywood was boarded up, the shutters
nailed together. Eneas, with an Indian carrying his belongings, walked to the bus for Ambato and soon was gone.

But the tragedy of Eneas repeated itself in Baños soon
afterward, with disturbing similarity in details.

When one walks under the big tree on the plaza and looks
into the water, one sees a small red flame burning in the
water. It is the cloak of the Lord who sits outside the old
church. He faces the square on a small table covered by his
fiery velvet cloak and shaded by a small and broken black
umbrella.

His face is cut out of polychrome wood; the agonized
glass eyes are turned heavenward; his mouth is half open,
showing a row of small real teeth behind his blue lips. His
body is a ghastly mess of wounds and running blood. He
is covered with them all the way down to the toes, which the
Indians kiss all day long.

The statue is not without merit; it is Spanish baroque,
vulgar, done in the spirit of butchery, but the modeling of
the face, hands, and feet is exquisite work. It is very old.

On the poor head, above the crown of thorns, they have put a wig taken from a doll, a wig such as Shirley Temple dolls wear. Two long flaxen curls hang alongside the face, the rest down over the cloak in back. At the feet is a strong-box, and from the shoulders on a string dangles a sign which asks for alms: "Give me something for my temple."

The Indians bend the knee before him, give him their coppers and realitos; but they love much more the Madonna who sits inside the church. To her they pray and sing, "Santa María, Santa María, salve regina."

Even for the *misa del gallo*, the earliest mass, this church fills up. It is an adobe building with some stone here and there, ordinary windows, and a low roof. It is a church only because it is blessed and has a bell tower, otherwise it is just a long room divided into a place for the congregation and spaces for the altar, the confessional, and a small stone pulpit from which the padre preaches. It is lit by candles which the Indians buy, and they also bring from the surrounding fields the flowers which decorate the altar— mostly large white, sweet-smelling lilies.

Besides the padre there is a sacristan, a trembling, chalk-faced, ancient frater who never looks up and always prays so silently that one hears only "s—s—s—ps—ps—s—s—s" when he passes.

The Madonna between the altar and the confessional is the statue of a beautiful young girl, without sorrow. She is life-sized, painted in the ever-fresh tones of church statuary. She wears a forget-me-not-blue cloak over a snow-white dress, she is smiling, and all in all she looks as if she had just come out of a bath. The Indians have been told that she arrived in the middle of a very dark night, riding on a black donkey. The animal with its sacred burden pushed open the door of the church and walked in. Inside, it trotted up to the sacristan's bell, took the cord in its teeth, and—dingaling, dingaling—rang it until the sacristan and the padre were awakened. The Indians love the story and must hear it over and over; the old sacristan tells it to them once a week, standing in front of the Madonna. On the back of the statue, pressed into the stucco of which it is made, one can read that the Madonna came from very far; it says there: "Gebrüder Pustet, Fabrik Kirchlicher Geräte, Leipzig" and "Made in Germany N° 186432."

The old church in Baños was built by the Dominicans. They had rented it to the Franciscans and these brothers were not very happy with the arrangement. They said to each other that Baños could stand a second church, and that it was folly to pay rental to the Dominicans.

Not far from the old church they decided to build their own. The new edifice was high and entirely of stone. It was lit by electricity, had three altars and six confessionals. The pews were of costly woods, elaborately decorated; there was a runner down the center aisle for high holidays, and windows of stained glass. The main altar housed in its lower part a relic of Saint Francis, and in its tower hung three new bells.

The church was opened with processions and ringing of all the bells—with every ceremony known to the church. Hot-air balloons were sent up bearing the image of Saint Francis. It was lit not only with electric light but also with hundreds of candles. A new organ installed in a proper choir played in easy competition with the leaky antique instrument that is hidden behind the altar of the old church.

The Indians came, wandered around in their bare feet, touched everything—with their hands and their eyes. They slowly took inventory of the new church, and then all of them ran back to their Madonna.

More resourceful and persevering than Eneas, the padres, who had noted the Indians' attachment to the holy Virgin, sent to Quito for one of the brothers who was a sculptor. He brought his tools and retired into the woods around Baños, where he began to carve a Madonna out of a seasoned piece of hardwood. One of the Indians, the one from whom he had obtained the wood, saw him and told the others, and when finally the Madonna was finished and set up in the new church, the Indians said, "Oh, no," and shook their heads; "that is not the real Madonna; our Madonna is in the old church. She came riding one night on a black donkey." Like children they remembered the story. Again they ran back to their church and asked the sacristan to tell it once more, and bought more candles than ever and decorated their Madonna with large bouquets of lilies and sang, "Santa María, Santa María, ora pro nobis!"

But even then the Franciscans did not give up. They reasoned that if Saint Francis, the Madonna, and Heaven did not help, perhaps the Devil would.

There arrived from Quito a large painting of Purgatory. It is one of numberless similar canvases that can be seen hanging in almost every large South American church. Baños until then had been without one.

Painted on panels which, when put together, form a picture twenty feet wide and eighteen high, it baffles the onlooker for a while with the maze of its figures. It is as obvious as a circus poster and painted in the same hues.

Framed in fumes and flames and in the upraised arms of
penitents, it depicts the Devil's holiday. He stands fanning
flames with green batwings attached to his shoulders; his
sweating assistants have the faces of black pigs from whose
fangs issue blue and yellow flames like those from a plumb-
er's torch. The catalogue of their amusements is a tiresome
repetition of cooking people, sawing them in half, pinching
and cutting up the rueful throng. Liars' lips are sewn together, thieves mutilated; and, to make it clear that this
torture is not ended by death, one of the devils is shown
driving spikes into a lecher's head, while the next one pulls
them out again. In the center of the tableau is a most in-
genious machine. The Devil himself is busy turning the
crank. Attached with thorny twigs to a large, flaming
wheel is a young, most carefully painted woman, altogether
nude. She looks voluptuous and her sinful lips are half
open; her flesh glares white in all the red, blue, and gaseous
colors around her. The instrument to which she is tied is so
built that as the Devil turns the crank, the girl's breasts
and abdomen will sail into a crowded arrangement of spikes,
hooks, small plowshares, and knives, which will disembowel
her. The last victim, from whose blood the knives are still
wet, is now at the bottom—an old bearded man, with the
word "Adulterer" written across his body, roasting over
an open fire.

Fortunately there is escape from all this. The sinners'
eyes are hopefully lifted to a high, narrow bridge at the
end of which stand two angels, one with a chalice in his
hand, the other holding half open the door to Paradise.
Beyond, half a mile inside Paradise, on a throne of silver
clouds, sits the holy Virgin surrounded by Franciscan

friars, with wings like angels, reading masses for the poor souls below and advising the Madonna for which of the sinners she is to intercede.

Hand in hand with the painting came a week of bell-ringing, processions, and exorcism. The Indians were there, all of them, and children were trampled as they crowded close to the picture. The padres explained it to them in detail—they asked to have the devils pointed out to them, and they listened to the story. The women sometimes left the church in tears, thinking of departed relatives and of their husbands' and children's future.

The padres granted reductions in the cost of indulgences, and lowered the prices of masses for the souls of the dead. It was possible to buy an amnesty of three hundred years in Purgatory for five realitos, and for a few days a thin stream of coins went into the treasury of the Franciscans.

All at once it stopped again, and the church was deserted. The sweet warm smell of the Indians, the revolting perfume of sweat and poverty, moved back to the Madonna. Soon afterward the new church closed. The doors and windows were bricked up, the old church inherited a bell and took a few of the pews. The great stone building stood forgotten; an avocado tree split its nave, and the fruits hang down over the altar. It echoes the cries of bats and of the small birds that are born in the electric light fixtures and in the tower.

The Franciscans left. Four donkeys, loaded with the eight panels of the picture of Purgatory, walked across the square and up toward Ambato.

9

The Ride with Rain.

On a Tuesday morning, shortly after the earliest mass, the truck from the Hacienda El Triunfo came up to the Gran Hotel Astor, and the mayordomo, Señor Rafael de Gangotena, sounded the horn several times. We drove off in a pink light, the sunrise reflected from a sky filled with small clouds. But first we had to stop at the Jefe Político's house to telephone our departure into the jungle.

Only a specialist can deal with the telephone here and send words over it. The local telefonista got out of bed and turned the little crank for a long while. With every feature strained he screamed into the apparatus, and then closed his eyes and held both earpieces to his head to listen. We sat down outside, and after a while the man came out exhausted and told the mayordomo that the message was delivered.

The telephone wire was with us as we went on. Beginning at the office in Baños, it runs over to the American Country Club, then to the side of the church, and along several telephone poles to the Gran Hotel Astor. Thence it is stretched over the pool to an avocado tree, next it swings loosely across the Pastaza, and from there on it follows the river, as the road does. The wire is old and camouflaged in greenery, and here at the beginning of the journey swallows are perched on it.

The road is wide and well built; the roar of water accompanies it to the right. This is the loudest river I have ever heard; it has the sound of a chorale played on tubas augmented by the sound of thin old wood breaking, of antique furniture being smashed.

Bridges are crossed, cars pass, the dust flies; and suddenly, after crossing three well-built bridges, the good part of the road comes to an end. Now it becomes narrow and hard to drive on, it crosses water again on a leaning wooden structure, and then it ends completely and turns into a mule path. Here is the Río Negro, with a few houses standing to left and right. Today the river is not black but of a light shade of green, which turns into white foam wherever the water is parted by a rock.

As the green water falls here, it is blown to spray that fills the valley. Wet leaves nod in the strong current of air that descends with the river. There is a whir and a rattling as in a bad cabin on a tramp steamer, a tumult deep down in the earth like the turning of an engine. Everything is moist, a kind of upward rain hangs in the air, a glow of small opalescent soap-bubbles, and the rocks and leaves are rinsed in blue and red and violet as the light strikes them.

The mayordomo put a poncho on a rock and we sat and waited here. In the river a little below the falls there are boulders, put there by design or chance, so placed that a man can jump from one to another and cross over. I did not think that mules and donkeys could do it. They came out of the forest on the other side after we had waited three hours and had stared so long at the water that the falls seemed to be standing still. They jumped across the river one after another and then, wet with spray, they stopped near the truck and the rock on which we sat. The aroma of their cargo arrived ahead of them, a sticky sweet and alcoholic smell. Each of the animals carried on a packsaddle two rubber tanks of a distillate made from sugar cane. The black sacks were sewn into hemp bags and weighed about a hundred pounds apiece, one on each side of the animal. As the donkeys and mules were freed of their burden and the sacks stowed away in the truck, a hideous stench mingled with the odor of alcohol. It came from the packsaddles and the blankets that went across the animals' backs, and from the animals themselves.

From the shoulder to where the saddles ended, each animal was covered with shiny sores, and a part of the spine was laid bare. In red and yellow wounds, suppurating and immediately black with flies, small ends of white thread twisted, wriggled, and crawled—fine worms a few millimeters long. The filthy pieces of sacking that served as saddle-blankets were smeary with the discharge of the wounds.

As the animals were freed, they threw themselves on their backs and rolled in the road. Then they tore at the grass and ate it as quickly as they could. They went to drink water; and in about two hours, when the cargo had all been stowed away, they were saddled again. Now they carried bags of cement, machetes, picks and shovels, and crates of stores. My baggage was wrapped in oilcloth and tied to the right and left side of a donkey, and then the first mule turned and started to cross the river.

In a long string the others followed, their ears up as they went from rock to rock. But soon they were trotting along in stupor, drunk with fatigue; there was no neighing from the few horses, no donkey brayed, and only the drivers who ran alongside were audible—forever singing the same string of curses.

The road swings up like a stairway alongside the Pastaza. It is so high up in an hour, and so close to the river,

that it becomes intestinally disturbing—it is as if you were
riding along the roof of a building on a road made of soap,
on a sleepy, stumbling horse. In this acrobatic undertaking
there is nothing to do but sit still and trust to the four
small hoofs. The river is so far below that it is no louder
than water turned on in the next room. There comes a moment when the whole scene begins to wobble again, when the
aerial road turns suddenly upward and inward, in four de-
cisive turns. The horse reaches with his hoofs—and you
wish he had hands—to get a grip on the muddy stairs; he
arches his back, pulls upward, and you find yourself about
five feet away from the brink and going inland.

The horse on which I rode, an unkempt pony, folded his
front legs as in prayer when we went down the next mountain. He took the curves of his own accord and all I had to
do was to sit still. The animal calculated, he knew exactly
how far to lean over to the right or the left; it is a breakneck
descent and at the bottom there is mud again. He was like
a snake at one moment and then like a frog; he crawled and
hopped, and we were down at the riverbed again and crossing the Pastaza. At the riverbank the animals piled together and had a few minutes' rest. Crossing one after another, they became cats, feeling with outstretched hoofs
under the water until they found secure footing and tried
to look down through the green current; then they moved,
steadied themselves, looked, felt, and advanced again, always standing diagonally in the strong current, the water
up to their chests.

A donkey here costs two dollars, a mule three. These
cheap, bad-looking, unkempt animals, all of them ill and
many of them with fetlock joints, win all your attention,

pity, and admiration. They are intelligent, resourceful, and brave, and they put you through a routine of fear, surprise, and gratitude that keeps eye and mind fixed on their hoofs and shoulders. There is nothing else you can look at on this first ride—a little patch of mud, water, a stone, or a bridge that appears around their ears just ahead.

In the next few kilometers a comparatively quiet passage followed, with only a few quebradas to climb down into and out of again. We came to a field with some banana plants and a few coffee bushes; alongside the road was a hut, and playing around it were several small black boars. It was the usual house, its walls made of split bamboo covered halfway with earth, an earthen floor and a cooking vessel, and the upper part black with smoke.

I observed what appeared from a distance to be a sweet domestic scene. Three people—a child, a woman, and a man —sat one behind the other and seemed to be arranging each other's hair. When I came near, I found that what they were doing was eating each other's lice. They searched for them with the manners and the industry of monkeys, parting the thick black hair, quickly taking the insects to lips and teeth and eating them. The group remained completely absorbed in their pursuits as the mules and donkeys passed them, and from far away at a turn in the road I still saw the three red ponchos close together.

We rode into the forest and then it began to rain. A lukewarm rain, dancing with gnats and mosquitoes; it doubled its pace a moment after it had begun and came in strings a few inches long. It changed the light, and everything became warm and moved closer together. It brought with it the stench from the galled backs of the animals, foul sweet air rising from the saddle as if it came from a heater, and above all else the smell of alcohol.

The water ran down from the sky as if a hose were being played on my hat; then it ran down over my nose; and after a while the inside of the hat got wet, and it ran to the shoulders, to the elbows, down to the horse and over the saddle. It weighed everything down and it was noisy. I wiped my face and shifted in my saddle and a new trickle went down inside my collar. The sound of the horses' hoofs was like pumps going, and all around water fell in sheets from the trees and flowed down over the large leaves. It bent strong flowers down until they emptied themselves and rose again. The saddle-leather stopped its twisting noises.

Sometimes the men whipped the donkeys and mules and they fought their way out of puddles and morasses into which they all but sank. We came to a swinging bridge, and here again they stuck their tired heads together and piled up, because only one at a time can cross. These bridges hang from wires that are fastened to rocks or trees or anchored into the ground and weighted down with stones. As the animal steps on the narrow slats of wood laid crosswise to form the floor, the bridge begins to sway and dance. Each new bridge has a different motion—some merely rotate, others follow the mechanics of a hairpin, with two periods of violent trembling before they come to a bend; some lurch upward and then slide off to the side and stand for a while like the roof of a house. Again the mules and donkeys were alert and had their ears up; they steadied themselves by bracing their front or back legs. According to the bridge, they would go forward with a rush on one, with a steady run on another, and creepingly on a third. Sometimes the bridges break and the animals drop into the river.

Toward late afternoon we climbed out of the low clouds. We passed some fields of sugar cane and for a long stretch the road was wide, smooth, and orderly as a park. There were waterfalls, and the perfume of plants and flowers, and a barefoot Indian passed, carrying on his back a large woven basket and a live giant ant-eater tied hand and foot.

In the wet green opening at the end of this part of the road stood a few houses, not enough to make a village. In front of one of the houses were some Indians and all the dogs of the settlement. I got off my horse and found them praying and standing around a chair, on which a child was sitting. The child was dressed in white, its hair decorated with silver wire and tinsel. It was a little girl, and she was dead. She must have been dead for a week; the face looked as if it had been rubbed in gray ashes. To make it sit up straight, a piece of the silver wire had been wound around the neck and attached to the back of the chair; the clay-like baby hands were folded together and tied with a rosary. There were vases of artificial roses, two candlesticks, and paper wings attached to the white dress. The dress, several sizes too large, was covered with lace and embroidery. The mayordomo explained it to me: the child, who is now an angel up in heaven, is kept as long as possible and rented out to relatives, and carried about in processions from house to house. This goes on until it is in such a state of decay that it can no longer be enjoyed. Then the child is finally placed in its coffin, with the words "*adiós, mamacita*" on the lid, and the properties are returned to the priest or the nuns from whom they were borrowed.

The parents and the relatives seemed completely happy

with this arrangement. There was little wailing, the mother was again in a blessed state, the little brothers and sisters and the father had someone to pray for them up above—and it is a chance to celebrate, to drink, and to praise God and Santa María and the patron saint of the little angel.

The knotted telephone wire that had followed us all the way made a turn here, and there was a river to ford, and it became evening suddenly, without sunset. We rode on; a brace of small green parrots balanced themselves on the telephone wire; there was a new forest and beyond this a bridge made of logs close together with earth stuffed in between.

Beyond these logs was a way station, a hut called the Hacienda Mascota, where we were to stay overnight. It stands in a large fenced field which serves as a pasture for the animals, who must feed themselves during the night. Inside is a room for the master when he travels, a bed covered with mosquito netting, a clean pillow and sheets and a blanket, a gun, and a locker with a strong iron padlock to which I had a key. In the locker was a can of sardines, a candle, ammunition for the gun, and a box of soggy saltines full of ants. I gave the sardines to Aurelio, who took them to the cook to open the can.

Meanwhile the cargo had been stowed away under the porch, and the mule drivers had gone to the open-air kitchen and brewed their yellow soup in a large pot—the national dish called "locro"—corn soup with potatoes, eggs, and red pepper. The arrieros sat in a long line around the porch; they fell asleep leaning against one another and against the house. In their ponchos, with their long, disorderly hair and beards, they might have been a tableau of the Apostles on Mount Olivet, except that all of them looked like murderers and stank of alcohol.

I walked out on the porch and saw my first jungle picture. Out of the trees, moving jerkily as if on strings, came soft, black kites with red ears. They directed their course to the pasture, toward the grazing animals, and hovered over them. They were vampire bats. They fluttered over the donkeys, mules, and horses unsteadily for a while, and then they drank. The animals stood quite still, without kicking or turning their heads: the operation must have given them comfort. The bats flew off a way and vomited the blood, and then returned for more.

I walked back to my room; I had to step over the mule drivers to get inside. From out of the darkness around me came Aurelio's voice. "The soup, patrón," he said. He had the table set and bread laid out, and a small lamp which he lit. The cook had opened the can and put the sardines into the soup along with the hard-boiled eggs and the potatoes. "Is very good," said Aurelio.

10

The Ride with the Long Night.

I drank some orange juice for breakfast at the Hacienda Mascota, and waited until the horse was saddled. Aurelio had run up to get the oranges from an Indian.

The mule drivers, loading their animals, looked more romantic than ever. They never wash themselves or comb their hair; water does not touch them unless they fall into it or get caught in the rain.

There were some rabbits at the edge of the field with little ears like those of bats, and someone had shot a deer with an old musket. The Indian who took care of the Hacienda Mascota showed me the antlers and explained that they are turned inward so that the animal can move easily through the dense forest.

Two soldiers and a prisoner arrived—the soldiers in uniform, with guns and shoes, tired and disgusted; the prisoner with a loose, striped convict suit and barefoot, light and happy. One of the soldiers introduced the prisoner as Señor Hector Espinoza. He was a bad and dangerous fellow, the guards declared, and had to be watched carefully. Among his misdeeds was a spectacular escape. He had asked the kind warden of the Panóptico in Quito to let him attend the baptism of his last child and the warden had given him permission to go with a guard. The prisoner told the guard that he would like to buy a little flour to make a cake for the celebration, and the guard took him to a grocery store, where he asked for a kilo of flour. He took the bag without paying for it and exploded it in the guard's face. By the time the carabinero could see again, the bad man was gone. They caught him a year afterward; he was sentenced and sent to the penal colony in the jungle; and now he was being taken back to the Cárcel Municipal in Quito, as a witness in the trial of another felon.

At night they tied him up; in the daytime he ran ahead and sang, and the two soldiers ran after him.

The three shared the sardine soup of the day before and then went on.

Outside the stockade of the hacienda lay a dead donkey. The caretaker of the Mascota had cut the skin and the flesh from him, and left only his head and the ears. Inside the ribs was a dog who growled whenever anyone came near to disturb his meal.

From there on, the day was like the first. The road went up and down, the animals swayed on bridges and wound their way a day's ride farther into the jungle.

About five in the afternoon of that day, Aurelio came close and pointed up into a tree. I had to look long and hard in the direction in which he pointed; so protective is the design that I would never have seen it myself. Some shiny green became a serpent, a sliding mass in all the other green of leaves: in the light greens, the dark greens, the saw-toothed green, and the deceiving shadows of palm leaves, a solid, dangerous mass of coils, it moved, slid, braced itself as if it had invisible arms and legs. The foliage about it trembled; a group of parrots flew past and then all was still again.

Late that day I noticed an increase in the echoes as the leaves and trees were suddenly without shadow, and then quickly night set in. It is like turning down a lamp. The trees change their form and take on soft contours, the green becomes slate-colored, and within it the small red fires of the wild orchids glow and then die. Tree embraces tree, and the things that grow downward and upward lose their ends and beginnings. It is all tired and caressing, it hums and chats awhile before going to sleep; and then new noises, small shrieks, yells, and deep bass voices take over. It breathes with a loud breath and even in the dark you feel that it is green here. An air root that swings from the branch of a tree comes out of the darkness, another one, invisible, touches your shoulder farther on, and then all at once it is as if you sat in the cabinet of a spiritualist, hung about with large sheets of black velvet that drink up all the light. You sit helpless in a bath of night; the saddle below you moves up and down, and through it you feel the horse, warm and walking, and imagine its head and tail and ears, but they are not there; nor can you even see your hands, though you bring them up to your nose.

Aurelio sees and the horse sees. Aurelio comes alongside and says, "A tree, patrón—watch out in front of you," and then I lie down flat over the saddle and there is a tree, a low arch across the road; I think I am going to bump into it, but it brushes down my back like a moldy sack.

"Look out, patrón, a bridge"—and look out, a river; the bridge sways, the river is wet. Farther on there is a cool current of air on the right, and then comes the sound of water running in the next room and the horse goes slower and has his head all the way down. He has pulled the reins forward and I know that under my right stirrup, with the smallest margin between us, is the river far below.

The horse is drunk with fatigue; he makes a false step, stumbles over a root, and you almost hear the angels sing; but that also passes, and awhile later, farther on, at a point where we come out of the forest, all at once—as if someone had thrown a burning coal on the black velvet—there is red light, a glowing stove hung in the sky; and silhouetted against it is the outline of the volcano Sangay. The road is visible now, and the scenery reminds you of a tropical cabaret in which everything is lit by red lanterns; and so it continues to a small village with a church, a tailor with his Singer sewing machine and charcoal pressing iron, a small shop, and a hotel with a bar.

Here the jaded animals were dismissed again, to seek their food in the dark. The mule drivers had a place to sleep somewhere and the mayordomo waved to the hotel—it has just "Hotel" written on it, no name. The electric light here burns from six to nine. A Salesian padre was walking up and down with a man in riding boots, and the proprietor of the hotel received us with many compliments. I bought a box of saltines and a can of sardines, the only available food in the store, opened the can myself, and retired into a quiet corner in back of the house to eat them.

Aurelio carried the saddle and bridle upstairs, and I asked the Spanish proprietor for a room. He said with many fine words that he was delighted, and to take the room on the right upstairs, in which already two caballeros had put their belongings. The mayordomo was also put into this room. I asked him next for a washroom, and he ran to a door a few feet away, opened it, and gave me a lamp: outside was a large field with trees around.

"Be not sad, patroncito," said Aurelio; "you must accustom yourself to this comfort."

I drank some whisky and walked up and down, and Aurelio walked a few feet in back of me; and then the electric light was turned off in the street, and we decided to go to bed.

Upstairs we found the two caballeros asleep in one bed, and the mayordomo and I were to take the other. "I like to sleep near the wall," said the mayordomo. The bed was an arrangement of boards with a thin, beaten, and filthy mattress over them. The snoring caballeros had covered themselves with blankets; a smoking petroleum lamp stood on a box, and the windows were without screens. Señor Rafael de Gangotena closed the shutters, and when I asked him why, he drew his finger across his throat and told me that across the river was the penal colony and that sometimes the convicts escaped and murdered travelers.

He then barred the door with the chair, put his revolver next to his head, spat out of the bed in a curve onto the floor, turned over, and went to sleep. Immediately the air in the room was like that of a crowded saloon; a soggy wet heat rose from the floor, moved out from the bed and the walls, and came down from the ceiling.

The walls of the room were papered, and after having quietly opened a window, I took the lamp and sat down on a box to read. The walls were papered with copies of the *Schweizer Hausfrau*. The first article that I came to was one of a series on good manners. The author seemed to be troubled in that installment by the problem of what to do with a lighted cigar. "What to do on meeting a lady"—the article began—"while walking along the street, wearing a hat, carrying an umbrella, and with a lighted cigar in one's mouth:

"When one carries an umbrella in one hand, has a hat on one's head and a lighted cigar in one's mouth, and meets a lady, one naturally takes the lighted cigar into the right hand, moves the umbrella up over the arm, then takes the cigar and puts it into the hand that holds the umbrella, thus leaving the right hand free to remove the hat. One can also stop and say a few friendly words to the lady. Under no circumstances does one leave the cigar in one's mouth while talking to the lady, even while removing the hat. Of course no one will be so rude as to come for a visit to a lady with a lighted cigar in his mouth."

An exchange of letters and several personal notices followed this useful advice.

" 'How can hemorrhoids be quickly and thoroughly cured?' asks a young woman, Mrs. S. H. of Rorschach. ANSWER: 'Hemorrhoids are cured quickly and thoroughly and most easily if for three or four weeks you eat two oranges a day. After a few days of this cure the hemorrhoids will begin to shrink and in fourteen days they disappear completely. Wishing you success [*Guten Erfolg wünschend*]'—Frau Lehrer Dubeli, Zürich."

"On account of death, for sale: 3 bird cages, 1 apparatus for perspiring in bed [*ein Bettschwitz Apparat*], a leather sofa in good condition, and twelve easy lessons in French."

The last article in this group was a melancholy announcement by Herr Lehrer Kläui in Brüggen, near St.

Gallen, who offered to educate unruly boys and guaranteed success.

When I looked away from the last line, I saw a swarm of insects sitting around me. They came in through the open window and flew into the lamp. I closed the window again and killed the mosquitoes and beetles; the dead bugs lay on the table and the chair and on the floor. And then I fell asleep.

11

The Day with Hunger.

The two caballeros 'were still snoring at the Swiss wallpaper—at a part where some poems by Hölderlin appeared in a Sunday supplement—and the door was blocked by the tilted chair. Through the cracks in the floor came smoke.

I went out to see if the hotel was on fire. The smoke rose in a twisted smeary column from under the building. The hotel stood on long poles, on which two monkeys on strings slid up and down, and the kitchen was under our room. A woman cook was below, barelegged in stockings of mud, a parrot on her shoulder and at her feet an assistant who fanned the flames.

As usual Aurelio had slept on the floor outside my room. He stood up in his poncho and disappeared to get our horses. An old proverb here says that half the journey is getting out of the inn.

The mayordomo was next to appear and ordered breakfast for us both.

A table was set on the veranda of the hotel. Out of a closet came a tablecloth reserved for distinguished guests; it was egg-stained and tomato-spotted. A handful of tinware, forks, and spoons, were set down. The mayordomo put his revolver next to his plate and looked in the direction of the oven. The cook brought milk and coffee. Here in the land where some of the world's best coffee grows, if you love coffee you must bring your own and a percolator besides. In Ecuador and the rest of South America, in good and bad hotels alike, they cook the coffee long in advance, brewing a foul ink of it, which is cooled and kept in a bottle. Half a cupful of this dye is poured out, the sugar bowl emptied into it, and a little warm milk added on.

The mayordomo ate and drank and asked me why I did not eat. I had an omelet with tomato in front of me, and although I was very hungry and had not had a proper meal for days, I had no intention of eating it. I had wiped my fork and spoon and was starting on the cleaner end of the plate, when I looked across the square and saw a butcher stand. There under a big tree stood a wobbly box. It was covered with tin, an old oil can cut in pieces and nailed over it. An Indian woman with a baby tied to her back stood next to the box with a leg of mutton in her dirty fingers. Overhead was a cloud of flies, so thick that you could reach into it, squeeze a fistful together, and throw them away. The woman had a machete and with this she carved the meat, the way you sharpen the end of a fence post. I sent Aurelio to buy two bananas for my breakfast.

For short intermissions we came out of the forest and then we rode into it again. The jungle has doors—like entrances to greenhouses. Outside there is a wall of earth, thickly covered with a rug of small leaves that resemble laurel. Sunk into these, solitary and apparently stemless, are little flowers, gentians. Then you come to an arrangement, bright as traffic lights, of pretty shrubs with tubiform flowers, copious reddish blossoms; and the chalk-colored blooms of geranium trees stand high in back. From a stagnant pond, crowded with weeds and small fat plants that resemble watercress, the black limbs of dead trees reach out, and on them sits an army of flies, bugs, and beetles in the colors of sulphur, arsenic, and copper.

There are rows of ferns on the green band of the wall,

their compound fleshy fronds stuck into the turf; and then you are inside and a botanical monotony begins.

Against the flat green-gray curtain of the background soar the trees, and the parasites that grow out of trees. In this steam bath are acacias, odoriferous flowers, yellow with binate spines three inches long, and fern trees with lacy leaves six feet in length. Bushes also grow on the trees, and everywhere are orchids.

From under our horses' hoofs came clouds of butterflies, some white and some with the pattern and color of mock turtle soup on their wings. After a while the very large orchids took on the shape of immense sauce-boats standing and hanging in the branches. Under them were huge leaves that had decayed or been toasted crisp brown; they began to resemble filets of sole cooked in butter—the very brown ones like pompano cooked in a paper bag—and the orchids, which were a strong fine yellow, seemed like dishes of mayonnaise.

I smelled other cooking too. It seemed as if invisible cooks were hidden in the jungle, and with painful, accurate detail of shape, color, and taste—and, above all, smell—held dish after dish under my nose only to take it away for a better one. I dreamed an immense bill of fare for the next few miles, a nightmare that began with assorted hors d'œuvre: céleri rémoulade, saucissons d'Arles, the hams of Poland, of Virginia, of York, of Westphalia, of the Ardennes and Bayonne, the choucroute garnie, the Tiroler Bauernschmaus. Then the soups: vichyssoise, germiny à l'oseille, onion soup au gratin, and marmite with marrow dumplings. The fish course followed: swordfish steaks, shad and roe, clam pan roast, cold barbue, and cold salmon.

Confusion set in after this: hashed brown potatoes mixed with ham and eggs appeared. Pâté de foie gras, mackerel in tomato sauce, Bismarck herring and other agreeable pickles, bouillabaisse and pilaff with chicken livers, curry and chutney and Bombay duck, canard à la presse, and a tray of assorted cheeses—Camembert, Brie, Pont-l'Evêque, Roquefort.

After I had gone through all the bills of fare, I thought of restaurants and their proprietors, their décor, doormen, potted palms, white and gold interiors, cherubs, orchestras, coat-racks, and of their service good and bad.

Of the vulgar tubs of butter at the Reine Pédauque, of the Restaurant Numa back of the Madeleine and its stacks of escargot plates. Of the big places in Copenhagen and Rotterdam with the red carpets, the immense waiters, and the terrines of soup in which, under a lake of melted butter, asparaguses thick as thumbs swam around. The carpets were dark as oxblood, and the people with stiff napkins tied around their necks sat eating for three hours. And Tirol, and hunger from skiing, a different language spoken at every table in an inn as remote as the little Flexen in Zürrs; the Salontöchter in the Swiss hotels, the stew made with Steinpilze, the peasant women who brought the little strawberries down from the fields. The restaurant in the basement of the Grand Central Station in New York, the part with the counters on the right, where you are served by waiters who rank second in gruffness and bitter faces only to those of the Lafayette, but where you get the best ham and eggs in the world, and seafood and stews that are rare.

The Chinese restaurants; the Grotta Azzurra in down-

LUCHOW'S RESTAURANT ON A SUNDAY EVENING

town New York in a cellar with horrible murals, mostly frequented by political rabble, where they cook lobster with small Italian plum tomatoes and where a waiter who looks like d'Annunzio brings you half a dozen napkins with the lobster and three plates for the empty claws and shells; and then, a little farther uptown, Luchow's. . . .

When I am in New York I usually cross Fourteenth Street and revolve the door of Luchow's on Sunday evenings. It is then that a small private miracle takes place. I sit down and watch for the arrival of occasional and peculiar guests. Where they come from I do not know. From a museum down the street, I think, where they are prepared for this visit with infinite care, where the men's noses are painted red, and the thin blue veins of too good living are etched on their cheeks; where antique Prince Alberts are taken out of camphor and brushed.

Here I have seen a Schubert and two Brahmses, and on their arms lovely old Winterhalter ladies. One man who comes is a Lenbach portrait of Freiherr von Menzel the court painter, and another looks like my friend, the eighty-year-old K.K. Hofschauspieler of the Munich Theater, Konrad Dreher. For their entrances, the orchestra fiddles through forgotten Waldteufel music. It is sad and *hausgebacken;* it seems as if outside, instead of the bawdy street, there should be the stop for the green and white trolley-car to Nymphenburg. The years of hopelessness and disgrace that have changed all this seem but a cloud of cigar smoke, rheumatism, beer, and Kalbsbraten.

At about that part of the restaurant dream my horse stumbled; I woke up and began to smell cooking—real cooking. We came into a clearing again and I hoped that we might be near a small hacienda which perhaps belonged to someone who had a chicken on the fire, or that we were at least in the vicinity of the hut of a Salesian padre—these good men sometimes cook for themselves. Between two large walls of earth, we saw a native hut from whose neat chimney smoke was rising; there was also some promise in washing that hung in the sun to dry, and in a well-fed dog.

I slid off my horse and found an oven at the back of the house, where an Indian woman was busy with food. She had a friendly face and she was reasonably clean. There was soup on the fire and she was busy cleaning out a monkey. She cut him up, going inside him with her knife, turning over the blade as if stirring stomach, liver, lungs, and then emptying him out. She singed off the hair and cooked him over an open fire. Another woman and a man came and sat down, and they ate the monkey, the man taking an arm and starting by eating the inside of the palm. He nibbled at the fingers and spat out the nails. The woman bit into the ears first. It was like eating a baby. My hunger was gone— I got on my horse and rode away.

Rafael de Gangotena came galloping back to me and wondered where I had been, and he said that we would be at the Hacienda El Triunfo in half an hour. He warned that ahead was a deep ravine bridged by two trees with earth stuffed in between, and said not to worry, the horse knew the bridge and would walk across and just to let him go.

The bridge came, and after it the hacienda. We were met by Don Antonio, the oldest son of the owner.

What music there can be in the sound of bathwater running into a tub, in hearing a cocktail mixed; and what pleasure in a simple table laid, and a bottle of wine in a bucket. There was even a bathtowel, a clean one, and a cake of soap.

This Is Romance. The Hacienda El

Triunfo reaches over several mountains and up into two valleys. It is bordered by three rivers and most of its ground is cleared of jungle. The trees have been cut and left lying where they fell; a wide stretch of land is planted in sugar. It grows and then is cut. The sugar is taken to a shed where it is put through rollers that extract the juice. The juice runs into large vats where it ferments; into stills where it is turned into alcohol.

The alcohol is poured into rubber sacks. The sacks are carried by mules and donkeys to Río Verde. From Río Verde the truck takes them to Ambato, to the office of the Estanco de Alcoholes, where a Government inspector takes them over. It is bottled, flavored, and sold to the Indians. A very simple arrangement that leaves a nice profit to the state and to the owner of the hacienda.

Labor is cheap, mules are cheaper; the one costly item is the machinery. When the sugar press has to be replaced, most hacendados would buy an American one, but the Krupp works offer one just as good for half the price and worry about installation and replacements.

The motor that drives the rollers, however, is American. It is an ordinary Willys Knight motor, taken out of a used car. Its owners speak of it with respect and affection as if it were a person. The motor was carried into the jungle in three weeks' time, the heavy parts by detachments of forty Indians. Since it was set up in a shack at the Hacienda El Triunfo, it has run five times around the world. Its speedometer is attached to it. It runs at an average speed of thirty miles an hour, day and night.

A group of boys, their hair, faces, clothes, and feet crusted and smelling like custards, feed the sugar cane into the rollers, and the sweet brook flows down a gutter through the roof of the house below. From this house comes the sweet alcoholic stench that fills the valley and attaches to everything that is here and trails out of the jungle with the mules all the way to Baños.

Some cacao, some coffee are grown here. There are a few banana forests, and experiments with California fruits— notably navel oranges and grapefruit—and with peach and apple trees are made here. This varies the green of the fields here and there; it is a private hobby of the owner. The money comes from sugar. It is extremely simple.

It all can be understood in ten minutes. At noon a siren blows. There is an eight-hour day, a paymaster, a doctor's shed, a breeding farm for donkeys and mules. The animals are fed the tender ends of the sugar cane, the juicy tops that are too small to press, and as long as they are young and not in service, the horses and donkeys are all fat and strong and healthy. Once they start working they wear out, and when they are through they are left wherever they fall and are replaced by new ones.

On a hill is the house where the owner and his sons live. One side of it overlooks the industrial part. On that side are the kitchen, the pantry, the store rooms, and the servants' quarters. The other side faces the jungle. The building is high up on stilts, and from the guests' rooms out over the land below hangs a wide veranda; leaning over it you have the sensation of looking from the bridge of a ship.

The walls, the partitions between the rooms, are made of split bamboo that is whitewashed. The beds are made of wood, the mattress supported by rawhide strips which are laced from one side of the bed to the other. In each room is a closet, a gun, ammunition.

A few yards from the house is a communal washstand with a shower bath. The shower is a barrel high up, filled by a boy who climbs a ladder. In this small house is also a bathtub. It smells of chlorine here and recalls the sanitary comforts of the barracks in army cantonments during the last war.

A cook and an assistant are busy around a small oven, and a boy waits on the table, wearing a white jacket when guests are present. The food is very good, with respectable French wines and an occasional bottle of champagne. Cocktails are served and whisky and soda.

In the afternoon the strip of the greenest green, that of the valley filled with sugar cane, is altogether like water, and then the illusion of being on shipboard is strongest. When it is evening, and the moon rises, a large improbable yellow signal, when Sangay colors one half of the sky red and the jungle exhales its peculiar and wondrous perfume, and the mists roll up against it, then it is theater.

On Altamir Pereira's shoulder at that moment usually sits his pet monkey. He holds onto his ears with his long cold fingers and repeatedly draws his cheeks back in short, fixed, and malicious grinning, and then he searches in the young man's thick black hair.

Altamir is dark and handsome, an aristocrat with a mole under the left eye, with enough brutality in his face to save him from being pretty. Into this musical-comedy backdrop he sings "You're the Cream in My Coffee," and then his favorite:

> This is romance,
> It's an omen of splendor,
> And you turn to surrender
> In a night such as this.
>
> This is romance,
> There's a sky to invite us,
> And a moon to excite us,
> Yet you turn from my kiss.

He goes through it stanza after stanza; he knows every word and pronounces it carefully. He has an old gramophone that is turned on most of the time, and he runs through all the Broadway moaning of the past ten years.

That night, after he had sung "She's a Latin from Manhattan," he turn. d and said, "Ah, American girls are standard—those legs, that skin. Ah, I don't know what it is, but no other woman on earth has it so much." He took a deep breath and sighed again and finished his song, his eyes half closed.

"Tell me about New York," he said. "Gee, the last time I was there, two years ago, someone introduced me to Joan Crawford at a party, in El Morocco, and to Franchot Tone. And here we are in this goddamn jungle. By God, couldn't you get me a job somewhere in New York? I'd do anything to get out of here."

The American songwriter, producer of musical shows and moving pictures, has nowhere more faithful followers than the youth of South America. Everything American is O.K. or swell or peachy. They have taken over all our slang words, some of them dated, and they love to speak in a Brooklyn jargon, talking out of the side of the mouth.

They know by experience that the beauty and the leniencies of the Parisienne are a fable, and they seem to think otherwise of New York. In nine out of ten cases, the locale of the small, transient ménages which they love to establish is in the neighborhood of Riverside Drive and the Seventies, around the Charles M. Schwab edifice.

Another favorite locality, dense with tender memories, is on the heights around Columbia University. The ladies in these episodes are always blond and beautiful beyond their power to say. They all are sweet, chic, completely unattached, and liberal-minded, and their names are handy, smart, easy to remember, like the roll-call of a musical comedy chorus.

The young men of wealth have access to the upper East Side, and to Long Island. They know the good restaurants, and their families stop in midtown hotels, usually in large suites together with their servants, whom they bring along. Two of the Pereira sons were born in New York, and they therefore refer to the Plaza as the Maternity Hotel.

The bamboo poles of the veranda vibrated all evening to the music of George Gershwin and Cole Porter. Into the night, like boys in a dormitory, they kept their conversation going through the airy walls. I had to listen to every word that Miss Crawford said that evening, to the details of a house party at Sands Point; and I had a clear picture of the charms and the anatomy of a dozen American girls.

Altamir was pale and wan the next morning. He said he couldn't sleep all night thinking about American girls. During breakfast an Indian came up and asked to see the

patroncito. The Indians here are decently treated and come
with their problems and requests direct to the master. There
are no Great Danes to protect him from them.

The Indian whined in the manner of a small boy asking
his mother for something he knows he will not get. He said
that one of his friends had just returned from Quito, where
he had worked at the British Legation, and that there at
the Legation they had what is called the English weekend.
He had talked it over with the other Indians and they all
agreed that it would be very nice to have the English weekend at the Hacienda El Triunfo. He had come to ask the
patroncito what he thought about the idea of having the
English weekend. The patroncito asked him to repeat
the story and then laughed, and the Indian laughed. The
patroncito put his arm around the Indian's shoulder, and
the Indian, laughing with all his teeth, said that he had just
thought it might be a good idea, and left. The problem was
solved—no English weekend.

We went into the jungle several times, on horseback and
on foot, at my request, and also to visit the headhunters.
We heard stories that they were very bad, and as many
stories of how good they were. It was laborious portage. On
the rides in the surrounding country we took a compass and
a bugle. Even natives get lost here; but we always found
the way home.

The jungle itself, once you are used to looking at parrots
outside a cage, and at orchids without a florist near them,
becomes fatiguing in its sameness—green, green, green—
water green, moss green, tree with green orchids, green tree
with parrots, fallen green tree—climb over it—monkeys

and their repertoire, repeated a thousand times with no variation in scenery.

The Indians that live along the roads, the workers and Government people and the whites, are unhealthy-looking, flabby, with yellow in the whites of their eyes and yellow in their skins; even the Negroes seem chrome-yellow under the surface. The teeth of all of them are bad.

You come occasionally upon a small store. The stock consists of ammunition for antique firearms, of Chiclets (you find these throughout Ecuador), of patent medicines all trademarked Bayer, manufactured in Leverkusen, Germany; cheap padlocks with the Yale trademark, also made in Germany; candies wrapped in tinfoil in very bright metallic colors in large glass jars; cans of sardines and herring in tomato sauce; whisky, chiefly White Horse, the seal broken and the whisky cut; and brandy, Marie Brizard and Hennessy, also cut; pictures of saints; crosses and candles; no newspapers, no magazines, no writing materials; a few pairs of shoes for men, and cloth for women; machetes; and buckshot in glass jars.

There are spare parts for sewing machines, for the American Singer and the German Pfaff. "To know how to repair a broken sewing machine is very important here," said Altamir. He could take any one of them apart and put it together again. The natives are as grateful for that as for the ministrations of a doctor.

We met a wandering photographer, a man with a box such as one finds in public parks, and a piece of sleeve attached to his box camera through which he reaches into it to develop the pictures while the subject waits. He had nailed photographs which he had taken all over the outside of the large wooden camera. Looking through them, I saw several girls who had had their picture taken with a sewing machine, in the fashion of people elsewhere who have themselves taken with a car or a horse.

On the longest of these trips we came to the settlement of some Jivaros, the headhunters of the Amazon. They were hospitable and friendly. We sat for a while on the floor of an elliptical house. Altamir spoke a few words of their language. We had to drink chicha. They seemed intelligent, their fields were in good order, the house was cleaner than those of any of the Indians around Quito. A boy performed miracles with a blowgun, shooting Altamir's hat full of holes. They allowed us to inspect their equipment, and they were all healthy and very clean.

The poison, the famous curare, with which they hunt, Altamir informed me, they no longer brewed, but bought from white traders. It came most probably from a chemical firm in Germany, he said. The only jungle note I could detect was the jaw of a vicious little fish, the piranha, which hangs next to the vessel in which they carry the poison. Before dipping the dart into the semi-solid fluid, they notch it with the teeth of this fish, so that the end is almost cut off. Monkeys, when hit, quickly pull the missiles out of their skin, and the poison would have no effect. As it is, the point breaks off, and the monkey drops down in a few minutes.

The women of the Indians we saw had surprisingly attractive and almost Castilian features; the men seemed amused, and continually smiled. I hoped to find a shrunken head, and I looked around everywhere, inside the house and in back, and under trees, as one would look for a forgotten canvas in a house recently occupied by a painter. But no-where was there a sign of one, or the sign of blood, or of any preparations. The household was in order, a complete set of pots and pans, of bed and baby clothing. There was no-where a man without a head. We said good-by to the Ji-varos, and gracefully and politely as Chinese they let us go.

Back at the hacienda's donkey farm, I made the mistake of admiring a young animal, and it was given to me as a present. Filomena was her name. She was pretty as a majolica vase is pretty, or a Spanish shawl, or a Massenet elegy; and at first she aroused the protective dislike that such prettiness always evokes. This had to be overcome.

Filomena was three feet high, with another foot of ears, all in wool as soft as a new chinchilla coat, with four white stockings and ebony hoofs. She wore a black mask across the face, and out of this shone her large, intelligent, and stubborn female eyes. All in all it was a costume for *A Midsummer-Night's Dream*, made to the specifications of Walt Disney.

I took her along with me when I left the hacienda and started on the way back to Baños. She danced at the side of the road in and out of the forest, and amused every-one with her caprices, with her sudden stops, her nervous hops to left and right, with falling asleep and with inquisi-tiveness that often ended in fearful surprises. She slept with Aurelio, and sometimes she ran ahead and at other times she came along after us. Altamir and I and Aurelio rode our horses close together.

We left the Swiss Hotel the morning of the second day, and came to the swinging bridges, over which Filomena had to be carried. She was light as a bird. And then we came to the aerial road, where the horses go down the three dangerous steps to a ledge that hangs out over the Pastaza's bed a thousand feet below. Filomena danced out of the forest and jumped and then she was gone. She kicked and turned, becoming smaller and smaller. I saw her fall for a long while and then she was out of sight far below us. I remembered the headline in Guayaquil: "YOUNG GIRL DESCENDS THREE STORIES."

"I have no gun, only a revolver," said Altamir, "and if I could go to a place where I could see her, I might not hit her with a revolver, only wound her. To go back for a gun is out of the question. I know you are sentimental about animals," he said, and repeated, "I have no gun, only a revolver. I cannot get down there; I would not go down for a man, even. What I mean is, I can get down, but I would never come up again. Neither would the donkey. Perhaps she is dead. If she is not dead, all her legs are broken. Good —so what will happen? Tonight, when it is dark, two green eyes come out of the leaves, and one smack of the paw and a little hot breath, big white teeth, and not much pain, and it's all over. The tigrillo will eat her up, and tomorrow Filomena is part tiger, a proud fate for a donkey," he said.

> There was a young lady of Niger
> Who smiled as she rode on a tiger.
> They returned from the ride
> With the lady inside
> And the smile on the face of the tiger.

We rode on, and after a while he started a long description of a blonde, who loved him for five weeks in Saratoga, where his papa went to take the cure. "Brr," he said, "cold up there in September. . . . You know what you could send me when you get back—a pullover. A pullover is very useful down here. It gets cold so suddenly. I feel cold now. Feel my hands."

13

Dream in Brooklyn. The road

coming back from anywhere is always much shorter than in
the first passage over it. Altamir Pereira rode alongside as
far as the Hacienda Mascota, excused himself once more
for inadequate hospitality and for the fiasco with Filomena,
gave me a list on which he had written the names of gramophone records he wanted sent to him and the size of the pullover. Then he wheeled his horse and rode back.

I came to a grotto late that day, a hollow room in the
side of a mountain large enough to put a cathedral inside it.
Its walls were lined with mosses and ferns, all of them wet,
dripping, green, and fresh. Bats, asleep, hung stored away
on the ceiling, and a mute column of dark, leaden water
flowed into basins of stone. Small lizards ran their fiery
patterns along the walls. At the stone basins two donkeys
were standing drinking, and an Indian was playing on a
flute. The donkeys were loaded with equipment, and between
them was a small one, as pretty and with the same coloring
as Filomena ; and except for the few hours of pain, the memory of the slow descent, it was a kind of resurrection.

It is one of the cursed things about owning a movie camera, or just a plain camera, that you cannot look at such
scenes quietly and leave them alone and go away. They cry
out to be filmed, particularly when they have color possi-
bilities. It is then that you have to get off your horse, find
the light-meter, measure the light, judge the distance, jump
from left to right, look back at the sun, check the light
again, measure the new distance, and then wonder whether

it would not be a more interesting composition from the other side.

In the meantime, the donkeys have had enough water and wander away, the Indian has stopped playing his flute, become interested in the camera and come closer to inspect it. When finally he is arranged in an interesting group with his animals, his face is frozen and without quality, the donkeys are clumsy, and all freedom is gone from the scene.

Furthermore, whenever something rare has presented itself on the street, in a bullring, at the door of a prison, on a mountain, or in the water, I have always found that my camera was either in the top drawer of my wardrobe trunk at the hotel, that I had used up all the film, or forgotten to wind the motor. I have promised myself again and again not to take the machine along, but again and again I do; and it is a disturbing and unpleasant companion.

I asked the Indian in the grotto to drive his animals ahead of him down the road. He wore a deep purple poncho, the road was like a zebra skin, slashed with lights and shadows, and I wanted to follow him awhile with the lens. After ten feet of film had been run off, I came to a curve and saw in my finder, sitting on a rock, Allan Ferguson. He was burnt black, he wore a poncho, and he looked even more distinguished in it than when he sat at the explorers' table at the Metropolitano in Quito. He stood up and waved. He had lost weight.

He was just resting a little, he said, and the Indian and the donkeys were with him. He had been six months in the Oriente, and he added in the crushed tones of failure that he had been looking for gold. He pulled a small vial from the pocket of his shirt and poured some gold into the palm of his big hand, two irregular nuggets, almost round, three worn, blunt fishhooks, and a golden nail.

"That there is gold in there is certain," he said, as if to excuse his presence.

He said that everyone who had gone in had found some, but no one had yet found the Valverde treasure.

Of all the golden legends of South America, the legend of the Valverde treasure is perhaps the most plausible and the only one that has rewarded those who have gone after it. At least they have all come back with a few dollars' worth of souvenirs.

The treasure is the ransom which the Indians collected to free Atahuallpa. Among all the old and faded papers that are guides to buried treasures—texts which have the cozy gurgling sound of a roulette wheel, and are also as full of promise as a prayer—the Derrotero of Valverde is among the most convincing. The document was written by the Spaniard Valverde on his deathbed and illustrated with a carefully drawn map made by one Atanasio Guzman, an unfortunate man, a somnambulist, who one night walked out of his house and fell into a ravine, where he perished.

The original Guide was stolen from out of the archives of the city of Latunga, and no one knows precisely when it was written. It is known that the King of Spain instructed the Corregidors of Ambato to search most diligently for the treasure. They organized the first expedition, and they were the first to return without it, having lost the padre who accompanied them mysteriously just on the spot where the gold was supposed to be hidden.

Allan Ferguson said that the Guide was simple and direct, and almost photographically correct, until one came to the end of it. He sighed deeply, hunched over his mule as he talked, his long legs almost walking along with the four feet of the animal. We had to stop at the Río Verde. A bridge had been washed away, and repairs were being made that would take a few hours. A little way from the river is a small house that serves as an inn, and here we sat down to rest awhile.

Ferguson searched in his saddle-bags and came back with the copy of the "Guide to the Valverde Treasure" and the Guzman map. He unfolded both, moved his finger along the text, and read it aloud to me:

"Placed in the town of Pillaro, ask for the farm of Moya, and sleep (the first night) a good distance above it; and ask there for the mountain of Guapa, from whose top, if the day be fine, look to the east, so that thy back be toward the town of Ambato, and from thence thou shalt perceive the three Cerros Llanganati, in the form of a triangle, on whose declivity there is a lake, made by hand, into which the ancients threw the gold they had prepared for the ransom of the Inca when they heard of his death. From the same Cerro Guapa thou mayest see also the forest, and in it a clump of *sangurimas* standing out of the said forest, and another clump which they call *flechas* [arrows], and these clumps are the principal marks for the which thou shalt aim, leaving them a little on the left hand. Go forward from Guapa in the direction and with the signals indicated, and a good way ahead, having passed some cattle-farms, thou shalt come on a wide morass, over which thou must cross, and coming out on the other side thou shalt see on the left hand, a short way off, a *jucal* on a hillside, through which thou must pass. Having got through the *jucal*, thou wilt see two small lakes called 'Los Anteojos' [the spectacles] from having between them a point of land like to a nose.

"From this place thou mayest again descry the Cerros Llanganati, the same as thou sawest them from the top of Guapa, and I warn thee to leave the said lakes on the left, and that in front of the point or 'nose' there is a plain, which is the sleeping-place. There thou must leave thy horses, for they can go no further. Following now on foot in the same direction, thou shalt come on a great black lake, the which leave on thy left hand, and beyond it seek to descend along the hillside in such a way that thou mayest reach a ravine, down which comes a waterfall; and here thou shalt find a bridge of three poles, or if it do not still exist thou shalt put another in the most convenient place and pass over it. And having gone on a little way in the forest, seek out the hut which served to sleep in, or the remains of it. Having passed the night there, go on thy way the following day through the forest in the same direction, till thou reach another deep dry ravine, across which thou must throw a bridge and pass over it slowly and cautiously, for the ravine is very deep; that is, if thou succeed not in finding the pass which exists. Go forward and look for the signs of another sleeping-place, which, I assure thee, thou canst not fail to see in the fragments of pottery and other marks, because the Indians are continually passing along there. Go on thy way, and thou shalt see a mountain which is all of *margasitas* [pyrites], the which leave on the left hand, and I warn thee that thou must go round it in this fashion ⌇. On this side thou wilt find a *pajonál* [pasture] in a small plain which having crossed thou wilt come on a *cañon* between two hills, which is the way of the Inca. From thence as thou goest along thou shalt see the entrance of the *socabón* [tunnel], which is in the form of a church-porch.

Having come through the *cañon,* and gone a good distance beyond, thou wilt perceive a cascade which descends from an
offshoot of the Cerros Llanganati and runs into a quaking bog
on the right hand ; and without passing the stream in the said
bog there is much gold, so that putting in thy hand what thou
shalt gather at the bottom is grains of gold. To ascend the
mountain, leave the bog and go along to the right, and pass
above the cascade, going round the offshoot of the mountain.
And if by chance the mouth of the *socabón* be closed with certain herbs which they call '*salvaje,*' remove them, and thou wilt
find the entrance. And on the left-hand side of the mountain
thou mayest see the '*Guayra*' (for thus the ancients called the
furnace where they founded metals), which is nailed with
golden nails. And to reach the third mountain, if thou canst
not pass in front of the *socabón,* it is the same thing to pass
behind it, for the water of the lake falls into it.

"If thou lose thyself in the forest, seek the river, follow it
on the right bank ; lower down take to the beach, and thou wilt
reach the *cañon* in such sort that, although thou seek to pass
it, thou wilt not find where ; climb, therefore, the mountain on
the right hand, and in this manner thou canst by no means miss
thy way.

"But you can miss your way. It's as easy as following a
policeman's direction down a set of streets to a jewelry
shop, until you get there, to the end where the hieroglyph
is. It directs you to go to the right, the map says to the left.
I went left and right, and I tore out all the weed '*salvaje*' I
could find. I put my hand in the stream, I waded in it, and
there I found the golden fishhooks, the nail, and the pills. Of
the tunnel with the church-porch I found no trace. For a
while I had a fever, and one night I shot my underwear full
of holes. I had it hung up to dry outside the hut in which I

lived, and I lay there for two days more, but otherwise I
lost no time. I was all alone—six months alone. But I didn't
mind. I always wanted to be an explorer and a prospector.
I mapped the whole territory.

"I did everything, I planned carefully, I took just this
Indian. I thought the more I take the more they eat. They
eat up all they carry. I arranged to be supplied in there
once a month. The trouble with most expeditions is that
they can't stay there. There's nothing to hunt, no fruits,
no Indians to buy from. Six months I was in there, all
alone."

He sat back, the corners of his mouth twitched, and he
unpacked his gold again. He brought out the little glass
bottle and spilled its contents on the table. It glowed in a
green light; his fingers dwarfed the golden pills and the
three golden fishhooks. He arranged and rearranged them
according to size and put the golden nail on one side and
sat and stared at them.

Men such as Allan Ferguson are terribly hard losers. You
find them as railroad station-masters, as artillery or police
captains, on the bridges of steamships and in pursers' offices. Their mustaches, when they wear them, are always
neatly trimmed, their eyes clear and honest, and their souls
in order. What they say is always true; they wear costumes
and uniforms with pride, march in parades, lead cotillions,
and join in singing. They have always wanted to be what
they are, and when all is right they are enviably happy. But
when the plan goes wrong, when their ships are taken from
them, or the wheels on their little wagons break, they are
lost and beyond help.

I thought that Ferguson would really cry. Hardly in

control of his voice, he put the golden fishhooks one by one back into the bottle, and he said:

"He's a Greek; he sold his small place in Brooklyn to go into partnership with me when I told him about the Valverde treasure. He's waiting down in Guayaquil. I don't know how I'm going to tell him. He thinks I'm a swell guy. He trusted me, he gave me the ten thousand dollars."

With a parting look of sadness he put the bottle with a string tied around it back into his shirt.

"Next time I'll go up on this side," he said, and pointed to the side of the mountain on his own map.

The disease is incurable.

14.

The Headhunters of the Amazon. On the fourth day out of the jungle, between the Río Negro and the Río Verde, we felt five distinct earthquake shocks.

We were sitting in a house to wait for a bridge to be repaired—another bridge. Our horses were tied to a fence outside. As the woman who was serving us poured two drinks into our glasses, a piece of the ceiling fell down on her hand, upset the glasses, and knocked down a bottle of whisky.

The floor trembled as if a herd of horses were running past outside; then, briefly, there was the sound of musicians plucking on the strings of violins. The woman ran out, her hands folded in prayer, whining "Santa María." Birds were in the air, the sun was shining, and the horses were gone.

Three telegraph poles weaved back and forth for a while; the wires swayed and then parted. The ends, like whips, snapped back to the poles to which they were attached. Two children had run up and were clinging to the woman, and all three of them were on their knees in prayer. The house did things one never would expect of a house. It moved like a person about to step out in a slow dance; like someone getting ready to take his leave, or making up his mind to sit down—undecided, half-finished gestures. After a while it settled down again. It held together, but all the perspectives of its doors and windows were changed. The show was over in about three minutes.

The men who had been working on the bridge were gone,

and the bridge was now beyond quick repair. We found the horses scattered and trembling, and rode up along the river to look for a ford. Some distance above, we crossed through the white foam, and descended on the other side to the Pastaza road again.

In the light green fields of sugar cane ahead, there appeared an hour later the roofs of the Gran Hotel Astor, the Hotel Free Air, the Pension Suiza Alemán, and also the three steeples of the two churches of Baños, all intact.

Now, coming out of the jungle, the Gran Hotel Astor seemed beautiful and important to us. It stood exactly where it had been, white and simple. The screams of the proprietress sounded from the kitchen. With its electric lights and its two bathrooms, it was a very comfortable hotel, and while we were away it had undergone some changes.

Two boards had been placed across the copper-tinted morass that oozed from the swimming pool, and over these, carrying a breakfast tray in her hands, walked Luz María, the child of nature. She advanced in a new and difficult gait, and when I called her she turned the way soldiers do when they practice right- or left-about faces. I looked at her feet and saw that she had shoes on. She glanced down at them quickly and smiled, and walked on with the sound of someone nailing two planks together.

In sympathy with the hotel, nature also had changed. A benevolent upheaval had taken place. The waterfall that dins into the ears of everyone in this valley all night had moved some fifty feet to the right of where it originally came down. Its old bed remained as proof, a slimy band hanging down the mountainside.

Where the untidy yard of the hotel had been, a brook now flowed, bathing the roots of several rotted trees. These had been carefully festooned with lianas and orchids, and the blackness of their trunks was offset by large-leaved water-plants. A screen of twenty-foot palms cut off the road, the service entrance to the hotel, and the bathhouse that stood next to the hot-water pool.

Out from under a swinging bridge, carrying a maze of air roots in his arms and a hammer in his mouth, an Indian appeared followed by a second dragging the trunk of a palm tree, and a third man, dressed as a ship's carpenter, carrying the leaves that belonged to the tree.

I walked into the hotel and found at one of the doors a pair of short, fat, yellow boots, the kind that no one but Cyril Vigoroux would wear. Next to them stood a tripod and an old movie camera, two cases of whisky, and a trunk with "EXPLORA INC." stenciled on it.

Luz María clattered in, her face filled with responsibilities. She stopped an instant, doing another about-face, to explain that an explorer was here, and that he was making a moving picture of the Jivaro Indians.

"I think I'll call it 'The Land of Nadi Nadi' or 'Heads Off'; but the title is not important," said Cyril Vigoroux. He pinched his left cheek, quickly and several times. A fly had bitten him there: the red blotch looked as if he had rouged himself.

He sat cross-legged on a packing case in a pair of boots identical with the ones that stood outside his room. He had six pairs of them, he explained, made especially for him. He was fast as a carp, in an open shirt, an old man with large breasts and a beard. He excused himself, brushed some dirt from his sleeve, and rushed away in his sun-helmet, bush jacket, bulging khaki knickers, and awful boots.

"Julie," he cried into his jungle, "oh, Woodsie, do me a favor!"

From the green depths of his plants he turned, pushed a banana leaf out of his way, and shouted that luncheon was at one-thirty on the dot, and to bring his old friend Allan Ferguson along.

"Julie," he cried again, "oh, Woodsie, where are you?"

Cyril Vigoroux had taken possession of practically the whole hotel. He had divided it into store rooms, offices, living quarters. He had also had signs put up forbidding you to spit on the floor. I got the room I had occupied before going into the jungle. Ferguson went to the Pension Suiza Alemán.

I wanted to lie down and rest, but the bed was not made and rest was impossible. The hotel was in a fever. Luz María clumped up and down, the carpenters hammered and sawed, all the stairs creaked, and doors were continually being opened and closed.

I then thought of taking a bath, and Aurelio ran for some towels; but a bath was also impossible. The tub was occupied by a bird. He was very beautiful, tall and snowy white. His single blue-gray leg stood in three inches of water, and all around his foot lay dead shrimp. A few of them floated in the water. The bird showed no surprise or other emotion. He appeared to be stuffed, and I thought at first of taking him by his convenient neck and standing him outside in the corridor while I took a bath.

But then I saw life in him. It was in his eyes, though not in the eye itself. The eye was like a disk cut with a precise, hard tool—several circles, one inside the other, the innermost the core of a target filled with blackness, and around it a wheel of luminous watercolor gray. At long intervals, with the brief efficiency of an optical instrument, he flicked the lid across his eye like the shutter on a speedy camera, the only sign that he lived.

Suddenly, and again mechanically, his white body had moved to the other end of the tub. From under the feathers a second leg had unfolded and with it he had spanned the length of the bath. Near the hot and cold faucets he stood still and wiped his glass eye with his lid. I left him there.

The corridor of the Gran Hotel Astor was crowded with groundsheets, eiderdown sleeping-bags, canvas buckets, guns, letterfiles, and several packing cases, all of them numbered and stenciled: "EXPLORA INC., CYRIL VIGOROUX." One large one was labeled "Tongue Depressors" under the doctor's name.

The child of nature came climbing up the stairs like a skier up a mountain. She turned painfully and then knocked on my door to say that luncheon was on the table. Allan Ferguson was already there. He was seated next to a blond girl. Cyril Vigoroux, who came running, introduced her as his discovery and star, Miss Claire Treat. It was the girl whom he also called Julie, and sometimes "Woodsie." Julie was her real name.

"I'm the outdoor type, 'woodsy,' you know," is how she explained it.

Miss Treat managed to look at the same time like a little girl and an experienced, easily accessible companion. Her face was divided into lovely details; after thorough searching for faults you found she was still beautiful, perhaps too

beautiful. It sang all over her, and you only feared that
when she got up there would be some painful compensation,
the disappointment of a bad walk, a sway-back, or bandy
legs.

She was, at the moment lunch began, displeased with her
hairdresser, a youth from Quito.

"The minute he put the first pin in my hair, I knew I was
stuck," she said. She turned her head slowly as if it were
on a turntable and showed a perfect hairline, lovely ears,
and curls hard and even as if glue had been poured over
them.

Allan Ferguson sat quietly. In an hour's conversation,
he said yes and no several times; that he loved to dance, that
he had been in the Oriente for six months, that he had taken
a warm bath at the Pension Suiza Alemán that had lasted
for three hours, and that tonight he would walk around for
another three to enjoy the sight of houses and electric
lights.

No one paid much attention to the fourth man at the
table, Lucien Tirlot, the young leading man. He played the
role of a doctor, and had previously been a landscape gardener in Miami. He carried Miss Treat in and out of all the
quebradas in the neighborhood of Baños. He rescued her
from the jaws of crocodiles, and hung with her from preci-
pices. He had been selected personally by Cyril Vigoroux on
account of his faultless profile. He cut woodblocks of the
Indians in his spare time, but disinfected himself thoroughly after every contact with them. For most of the time
he sat in the shadow of a great tree, named after the famous
Ecuadorian poet Montalvo. He leaned there on his right
hand and the left hung down out over his knee. He used up

all the bathwater at the hotel. During luncheon his eyes were on his hands; occasionally they swung up to Allan Ferguson.

Doctor Vigoroux talked most of the time. He detailed the aims of his organization. The alert doctor's business affairs were most involved. Not only was there the film, which he directed and for which he had written the scenario. He was burdened with "tieups." He had, he said, a tieup with a cigarette concern, and one with some sleep-inducing coffee people. He was tied up with several publications, zoological, geographical, and of interest to travelers and explorers.

He was after the largest boa in the jungle and almost had his hands on it. As soon as the Indians produced this snake, he had it tied up with a lecture-tour management, nation-wide in scope.

He had Claire Treat tied up, and also a tieup with a steamship company. But the greatest tieup was with the group of Jivaros who sat outside in the yard of the hotel. These he wanted to bring to America, to exhibit them shrinking heads. The heads of animals, of course—of dogs, cats, departed household pets.

The tieup with Miss Treat needed no explanation. She put two lumps of sugar into his coffee, broke the third in half, stirred the coffee, put the spoon beside the saucer. She did all this as mechanically as he kissed her hand about a dozen times during the meal. In between he pinched his cheek and looked around for the waitress.

After the coffee, Cyril Vigoroux told several old stories, none of them amusing enough. During this recital, Lucien Tirlot leaned over to me and asked whether it was true, as he had read in the Quito paper, that Allan Ferguson was really a Norwegian baron; and then he said that he thought he was a very striking man.

"I think he's wonderful," he added and sat up straight again. Claire Treat also examined Ferguson. She measured his hands and arms, and looked at his hair, his lips, and his eyes.

Ferguson sat erect, heroic, silent, and listened politely; and after Cyril Vigoroux had told his most ancient and most South American joke—about a padre and why he has a tonsure at the back of his head—we all got up.

Woodsie played the young girl. The long black lashes were down over her eyes; she could blush at will and the color had risen in her sunburnt cheeks.

Allan Ferguson pulled her chair as she got up. The big, brave man, with the horsy honesty in his countenance better established than ever, looked damp and clumsy.

Woodsie lit a cigarette—at least she brought out of her coat pocket a packet of paper matches. They were brilliant red, and printed with a large golden "21" and the names of the partners who own this elaborate New York restaurant. This matchbox served her as a small passport. It announced where she came from, with whom she liked to go, and what her pleasures were. It also lasted forever because before she could tear out a match someone was always ahead of her. That and a Lilly Daché hatbox were her proudest possessions.

Cyril Vigoroux led the way to his jungle, sat down on the stairs of the hotel, and invited us to watch the shooting of some scenes.

The Indians sat about waiting to dance, to shrink heads, and to be dangerous. Most of them were recruited from the hills around Baños, three or four of them with their wives and children. The ones that were always placed close to the camera were real headhunters.

Like animals that are kept in cages, the Indians during their confinement in the backyard of the hotel had become disorderly and unclean. They left the remains of foodstuffs about; filthy clothes were draped over the fences; and they sat close together under a washline from which a sloth hung, blinking and groping along the rope ahead of him, his unfinished face turning slowly left and right.

The Jivaros seemed not overly eager to practice their ancient customs, to dance and sing. Their war cries were half-hearted and the doctor got the proper performance only from the chief, whose wife was soon to give birth to a baby.

With great authenticity and attention to the smallest detail, this Indian had retired into a little dream ranch which he had built for himself out of chonta palms and large leaves. There he sat brooding, bent over in a cowering posture, in the kind of couvade that is often reported of the ancients and of primitive races, and frequently of the headhunters of the Amazon.

This couvade is a state in which the father takes to bed and receives all the delicacies and careful attentions that other peoples properly regard as the mother's. The remains of the desserts of the Gran Hotel Astor, the left-overs of rice pudding, of custard, of ice cream, were carefully scraped together from the plates after lunch and taken out to the low house of leaves. To bring this important domestic detail within the swift and sure unreeling of his story was one of the problems of Dr. Cyril Vigoroux. Meanwhile he examined the mother, and hoped that the child would soon be born, as the chief was badly needed.

Production had advanced to that part of the film where the enemy is killed and the tsantsa—the trophy to be shrunken—is severed by two swift strokes from the trunk of the victim. The warrior sits down and receives the juice of tobacco mixed with saliva from the chief, who blows it in through his nose, a ceremony which protects the warrior against the vengeance of the dead enemy's spirit.

Everything had been very satisfactory thus far, explained Dr. Cyril Vigoroux. A head had been obtained with some difficulty. An attendant at the morgue of a hospice in Quito obliged, since the Jivaros refused to bring one of their own enemies' heads. The face had been properly peeled from the skull and it lay boiling in a ceremonial vessel. The doctor fished it out with a stick. It resembled a dirty washrag with holes for eyes and mouth; a wrinkled part was the nose, and the ears were still attached at the sides. In the kettle swam large eyes of fat, as in a soup. It smelled of ordinary cooking.

Before they could continue with the shrinking process, which reduces the head to the size of an orange, the important ceremonial was necessary. The chief did not want to come out. The warriors protested through their spokesman that they did not wish to have the tobacco juice blown in through the nose, that they had never heard of this ceremony.

The spokesman reported back to them that it would not be tobacco juice but chicha, and they accepted this amendment. The chief, however, remained in his house of leaves and insisted on awaiting the birth of his child before he would take part in the ceremony. Dr. Cyril Vigoroux examined the mother again and said that in another twenty-four hours he hoped they could proceed.

In the meantime, in another chapter of the film, Lucien Tirlot was dragging Claire Treat through the jungle, and they came to the lagoon in back of the Gran Hotel Astor. The doctor had them rush on and fall face forward into the water, and then he had them do it over again. He finally decided that Woodsie should come alone. She leaned down in the posture of the nymph in the White Rock mineral water advertisements; she wore a carefully torn shirt, her hair was loose again, and Cyril Vigoroux waded into the water to make closeups of her heavy breathing. He stretched her out on a jaguar pelt, and then completely lost the thread of the story. The rest of the afternoon was taken up with lovely still lifes and the shooting of a crocodile. He said he had tieups in mind.

Dinner was at seven, and afterward Cyril Vigoroux came along for a drink at the American Country Club. He was tired, and he wanted to work on the next day's continuity, he said; so he walked home, and I went with him. Woodsie and Allan Ferguson stayed to dance, and as we came to the hotel, we saw Tirlot through the window making woodcuts.

The doctor's room adjoined Miss Treat's. It was a frugal apartment: the same cot as in all the other rooms, a piece of native rug in front of it, and in the center the electric bulb hanging at the end of its wire without a shade. There was a radio, and also a gramophone standing on a specially constructed trunk that held records, all of them classical, Sunday evening program music.

On another trunk which he used as a bedside table was a small bar with half a dozen bottles of liqueurs, all sweet: chartreuse, kümmel, benedictine, and such stuff. For his particular guests Cyril Vigoroux went to the trouble of making a pousse-café, pouring it so that the colors of the spirits remained separate, one above the other. It took patience and a very steady hand, and it made a horrible combination.

On a shelf above the bed was a smeary jar half filled with vaseline. A sprig of blossoms was stuck in it.

He looked at his swollen cheek in the mirror over the washstand and yawned, and then he took his boots off and put them outside the door. He pinched his cheek and sat down on the bed, rubbing his thick legs. He had to write half the night, he said, and yawned again; and then he remembered that he also might have to deliver the Jivaro baby.

Someone outside was singing above the waterfall's tumult, the Indians and the animals were quiet, and all was otherwise silent in the thirty-five rooms of the Gran Hotel Astor in Baños.

The walls of the hotel were thin, neither the doors nor the windows fitted well, and the ceilings on the second floor were made of mats nailed to the rafters. At midnight there was a sound of metallic tapping. I wondered for a long while what it might be, and finally remembered the bird. He was eating his shrimp in the bathtub.

"I don't like mystery boys!" shouted Cyril Vigoroux at three in the morning. "All this bunk about his father being a Norwegian baron—Christ, I can't stand all these phonies that come around here! You, of course, think it's wonderful. . . . Oh, my God, the way you look at him when you dance with him."

"What do you mean?"

"I mean dancing—hanging from some son of a bitch and going around in circles. I suppose that's fun, great fun. . . . Leaning up against a leg—I'd rather do it in bed. My God, the fun women miss by not knowing anything about music, good music I mean!"

"It's funny," said Woodsie in a new and competent voice. "It's funny that you always say things that apply to yourself—all this blustering and bluffing, and when anything important comes up, you sit there in a corner and wag your tail, when you really should speak up."

"What are you talking about?"

"You know what I'm talking about."

There was silence and then a few loud slaps, a scream, and "oh! oh! oh!" and then all was quiet again. A palm swayed outside, the bell of the church tolled four times, and out in the new yard of the hotel the moon shone on a broken barrel of green dry paint that was spilled over an old Singer sewing machine.

Vigoroux came up to the pool the next morning and sat down in the water beside me, and Luz María brought breakfast.

After he had stirred his coffee and before he drank it, holding the cup in his hand, he said, "Good God, I hate to lay hands on a woman, but it does them good sometimes. The fit she threw the first time I smacked her. I hit pretty hard; I hit her the left side of her face with the palm of my hand. She turned her head and I hit her on the right, good and hard.

"You know how little girls act the first time you thrash them; they can't believe it, and they gasp in surprise, say 'oh! oh! oh!' and then break out in screams. Well, that made me really mad. I turned her over and beat her until my hand hurt. She'll boast about it. They love a hiding, you know."

He drank some coffee, swam about in the pool, and asked me to put a plaster on his cheek where the fly had bitten him. Then he put on a bathrobe, slipped off his bathing suit, and ran back to the hotel.

An hour later he was silent. He was sitting cross-legged on one of the rotten trees. In back of him lay the alligator, dead, that had been thrown there after filming the day before.

"She's gone," he said. "With what's-his-name. With Ferguson."

15.

Adolf in Quito. Luz María, in her
new shoes, saddled a horse, and I set out from Baños with
Aurelio. We rode to Pelileo and Ambato, to Lasso and Lata-
cunga, and back in slow stages by way of Machachi to
Quito.

Quito is a kind of penal colony for diplomats. In some
cases they are banished to this high capital for minor in-
discretions, alcoholism, badly conducted affairs of the heart
or the state, or—as a typist at the American Legation remarked of his superior—"because he hasn't got all the
marbles the Loh'd wants everyone to have."

This makes on the whole for a group of likable, out-
spoken, and refreshing people. Not being *persona grata*
with their own governments, they get along well with their
hosts, tell well-flavored stories, and are usually excellent
companions.

The German Minister is a delightful gentleman. No one
hisses him or tries to throw stones through the windows of
his house. Although six carabineros are needed to guard the
Italian Legation, no protection is needed at the German.
The Minister is a devout Catholic and goes regularly to
the cathedral, where he has to stoop to pass through the
portal, because he is so tall. He tries to hide himself at the
few parties he attends, and leaves before anyone has had
more than two drinks. If, in this land of surprises, the German Minister is a kind and cultured gentleman, it might
follow that a Jew here would endorse Hitler. As I discovered, he sometimes does.

I ran into Herr Doktor Gottschalk one day when he was

sitting alone in the back room of a place that might well be the German Legation—a whitewashed and brightly lit restaurant called the Salon Berlin. This establishment is a succession of vaulted rooms, somewhat like a rathskeller. The air is heavy with the stench of pickles and stale beer. Over a counter on which there are stacks of smoked herring and pumpernickel, a good-natured proprietor leans between a cash register and a sausage-slicing apparatus. The clientele is chiefly young men, standing straight, most of them in knickers and belted jackets, their hair clipped short, heavy-muscled, loud, and healthy. They are a group who used to do their best to look like typical Heidelberg students but now make every effort to look like mechanics on their day off. They are for the most part employed by German import-and-export companies. There is no picture of Hitler in the restaurant and no Nazi flag, but "Deutschland über Alles" and the "Horst Wessel Song" and all the brutal hymns of the new Germany are as popular here as the barrel of sauerkraut that stands in the outer hall.

When I arrived, Doktor Gottschalk was eating a pair of small sausages and drinking a glass of blond beer. I had met him once at the Hotel Metropolitano, and had been surprised afterward when someone told me he was a refugee and a Jew. The Herr Doktor is straw-blond, blue-eyed, professorial, and somewhat arrogant in his walk and his gestures. As soon as I sat down, he brought the conversation around to Hitler. He swallowed the remnants of the pair of sausages, took a deep drink of the Vienna Export, and started to speak of Adolf. He said the name as one does that of an old friend.

"I don't know," he said, "what Adolf had against me—

God alone knows. I am not like the others. You know, I was
in the field from the first day on in the last war—captain in
a line regiment, Austrian artillery, decorated with the Iron
Cross, first and second class, and mentioned three times in
army dispatches. I was being recommended for the Pour le
Mérite just when the whole *Schweinerei* came to its dis-
graceful end. All that counted for nothing, for absolutely
nothing." He said this in a tone of voice which seemed to
mean that he admired the thoroughness with which the new
government did away with everyone who was a Jew.

"My mother was an Aryan. Also, my wife is purely
Aryan; we have a son named Kurt—you should see them.
My grandmother was already *hoffähig* at the court of the
old emperor, and my father, the old Doktor Gottschalk,
personally treated Adolf's mother. All that means absolutely nothing. Can you understand what Adolf has
against me?

"My Papa," he continued, starting in on another beer,
"was in Ischl when he treated Adolf's mother. My dear Papa
was in the habit of keeping all the letters that grateful pa-
tients wrote to him. He had one from Adolf, a very nice
letter, thanking Papa for the care he had given his mother.
It was a long and elaborate letter, taking up two pages,
written on both sides.

"Papa was quite an old man when Adolf came to power,
and he was a famous specialist in Vienna when Adolf
marched in. Then the trouble began. Many of the others,
the old ones, committed suicide. We stayed home, and then
Papa thought of the letter—he thought of it when my
brother, who is also a doctor, and I were taken in protective
custody and when my little boy was forbidden to go to

school. He thought that the letter would do some good, and
sent it to Adolf through the proper channels. Adolf at the
time was in Vienna, and some influential friends who were
in the new government saw to it that it came to Adolf's attention. Papa waited and hoped that it would do some good.
It did.

"Adolf made it possible for us to get out of the country
immediately. My brother and I were released, we could take
our furniture along, and while everybody else had to stay
in line to wait for various permits, we left in a matter of a
few weeks. Our other property, our money, and my father's
and brother's and my own practice, of course, were gone.

"Papa, who is here with me, is now eighty. My brother
has gone to Chile. He is a gynecologist and has found an ap-
pointment at a hospital in Santiago. Papa was a famous
man in Vienna, and some time ago the Nazi Gauleiter of
Quito called up and said that he would send his wife over to
have him examine her. Papa got very mad, and he told him
over the phone that, according to National Socialist law, the
examination of an Aryan woman by a Jewish doctor was
equal to having relations with her and punishable under
the same law. She came anyway, and the Gauleiter, a very
nice man, came with her and laughed and said that the law
did not apply to Papa because he was over the age limit."
The Herr Doktor chuckled.

"But Adolf could have been a little kinder to us," he went
on. "There are several half-Jews in the government over
there, and even in the army. For example, Marshal Milch is
a half-Jew. There is a way in which to get around the regu-
lations. The Aryan mother goes and swears that while she
was married to the Jew, the father of her child was another

man, an Aryan, and in important cases that is accepted and
no more is said about it. If he had wanted to, Adolf would
have been able to make some such arrangement available to
us, but in the tension, and burdened with all the details and
all the worries he must have, one cannot expect him to
bother with any one individual case."

He touched my arm and pointed to a man who had just
come into the Salon Berlin and was being greeted with rev-
erence all around. "That," he informed me, "is the secretary
of the electric works and the local agent of the Gestapo."

The Gauleiter came over, shook the Herr Doktor's hand,
and walked on. The Doktor was visibly proud. He pointed
out other people to me, including one of the pilots of the air
line to Guayaquil, a baron. "The air line has become an
Ecuadorian company," he told me, "since all the trouble
with the United States began, but only five percent of the
capital is Ecuadorian. It's still a German company, and
when there's any motor trouble we have parts here from
Brazil like that." He snapped his fingers.

The Gauleiter passed us again and nodded. The Herr
Doktor smiled and said to me, "You know, they have been
very nice to us refugees since we are here. I went to the Con-
sulate the other day about some papers, and the secretary
there offered me a chair and said, 'Herr Doktor Gottschalk,
if there is anything we can do for you, turn to us with confidence. We have instructions from Berlin to extend to you
and other refugees any aid that is possible.' My son is even
going to the Colegio Alemán, the best school here."

The Herr Doktor had a nice house in the center of Quito,
and invited me to go home with him. On the way home, he
bought the *Comercio* and quickly read the headlines. "You

see," he said, "Adolf is no fool! Did you listen to that marvelous speech he made the other night about stopping the war?"

The house was orderly and the furnishings were those of a well-to-do German household. A picture of Hindenburg hung in the dining room, and a mediocre oil painting of an Austrian artillery battery hung over the Herr Doktor's bed, an immense featherbed which he had been allowed to bring over with him, along with all his books and the family silver and porcelain. The father, a white-haired and bearded gentleman who looked more or less like all great Viennese specialists, was in a wheelchair.

The Doktor's wife was the middle-aged, well-groomed German *Dame*, looking like a very young Queen Mary, German in the fashion in which many English appear German, a little rounder, a little more provincial, with a stiff high collar and a hard eye for the servants. The boy, Kurt, came in while I was there, clicked his heels, bent low and suddenly from the hips, as if about to kiss my hand, then stood at attention, a perfect specimen of the Hitler Jugend. He wore short trousers, for which he was already too old. They left exposed a good deal of sunburnt leg, covered by yellow down.

The Frau Doktor told me that a play was going to be put on by the students and teachers at the Colegio Alemán. It was a Nazi play, so Kurt, for obvious reasons, had not been asked to take part. However, he and his parents were invited to attend a dress rehearsal that afternoon, and the Frau Doktor suggested I come along. That evening, when the real performance would be given, only members of the

Nazi group would be admitted. After the performance in
the evening , the Nazis would have tea and cakes together at
the school, the Frau Doktor explained. "We, of course, are
not asked to that party," she added, with a look at her husband, "and what goes on there, and what is said and decided,
one can only guess."

Driving out to the Colegio Alemán, the Frau Doktor told
me that she was glad her boy would be here in Ecuador until
things became a little different over there. Today he would
be in a very peculiar position in Germany. There, it would
be better if he were a half-Jew instead of being what he is,
a quarter-Jew. If he were a half-Jew, he could obtain permission at least to marry a Jewish girl, but being a quarter-
Jew, he would be, according to the Party, too good to marry
a Jewish girl and not good enough to marry an Aryan, and
in consequence would belong to the unfortunate group that
is not permitted to marry anybody. "But that," said the
Herr Doktor, "might eventually be changed."

We arrived at the Colegio Alemán, which consists of a
clump of buildings standing in a large garden. There was
a Nazi flag, large as a bedsheet, flying at one end of a foot-
ball field. A kindergarten mistress, her hair pulled into a
tight knot, passed with some children, half of them Ecuadorian, the other half German. They wore the small aprons
that one sees in French nurseries. The buildings were im-
maculate. Over the door of each classroom was inscribed the
purpose to which the room was assigned—"Arbeitszim-
mer," "Lesezimmer," "Spielzimmer," "Speisezimmer." In
the kindergarten, a sun-flooded room containing very little
furniture, a life-size, full-length picture of Hitler hung un-

der a frieze of geese and rabbits. I asked the Herr Doktor whether this school, which was a public institute of learning in Quito, was a Nazi institution. "Not very much," he said. "The Herr Direktor is a very broad-minded man."

I was not permitted to attend the dress rehearsal, but I met the Herr Doktor the next day at the Salon Berlin, and he told me that the play was about an old Jew and that he was glad his papa had not been strong enough to go along. He and his wife and Kurt had sat through the whole business. He talked and talked, and then I went and talked to some others—half-Jews, quarter-Jews, full Jews—and I found in a number of instances more or less the same unbelievable and pathetic attitude. Out of all I heard, I gathered that many of the Jews in Quito—a city where nothing expected happens—feel like this:

"He'll rule the world, or at least Europe. In my case an error has been made. In the haste and hurry, the laws were made too strict. They had to be strict; you can't do things half-way. Too bad, but I shall be among those who will perhaps be called back. When it's over, he'll need every man— every doctor, every engineer, every scientist, every able executive. The soup is never eaten as hot as it is cooked. And then my Iron Cross, and the fact that I have kept quiet here, where I might have talked, and the fact that I have an Aryan wife and a child who is only a quarter-Jew—all this will make it possible for me to go back to the most beautiful, the best, the greatest land in the world. That's the reason I send the boy to the Colegio Alemán, so that he does not lose touch with the *Vaterland*."

And audibly my Herr Doktor added, in his soft Viennese German, "*Damit der Bua wenigstens was anständigs lernt.* —At least in this school a boy can learn something respectable."

16

Prison Visit.
Atop one of the foothills of Pichincha, high above the city of Quito, bathed in sunlight, stands a white building with a cupola. It is the Panóptico, and it has an evil name. Don Juan Palacios in Guayaquil had recited its horrors to me, and wherever I asked permission to visit the prison I was told with politeness and much regret that this one wish could not be granted. Diplomats in cautious conversation told me again that its cells were subterranean and wet, that the prisoners were chained to the walls, underfed, without proper clothing. Bony, feverish victims of political miscalculation, who died slowly, without consolation, and stank to high heaven. Lucky were they who were sent to exile in the Galápagos Islands or marched into the jungles of the Oriente; there death was quick and in the daylight.

The magnificent name of the prison and its story drew me up the hill, which I climbed in short stages of thirty paces at a time. For a while, when you return from the low lands, it is difficult to breathe in Quito, and you proceed by resting on a streetcorner, advancing thirty paces, leaning against a house and then a tree. Thus I arrived at the Panóptico.

Outside, propped against the building, were two sentries in khaki uniforms, with legs crossed, resting their hands on the barrels of their guns. They were talking and laughing; one turned, when the other pointed at me, and raised his eyebrows.

"I would like to see the Director of the prison."

Ah, he said, but that was not so easy; there had to be ar-

rangements made for this ahead of time, a letter, an intro-
duction, a pass, or else one had to arrive in the company of
an official of the Government, or at least of a policeman.

I told him that I knew all that, but that my visit was an
exception, that I was a prison official myself, from the
United States of North America, that I was the secretary
of the warden of a prison.

The soldier's eyes grew respectful and obedient, he leaned
away from the building, saluted, and dragging his gun behind him he almost ran up the portico to the door, where he
told the story to the man who sat on guard there. The guard
stood up and said, "But certainly, come in, come in, the
Director will be happy to see you."

Door after door opened. By the time I arrived in the reception room of the Director's apartment I had shaken
hands with several officials and rapidly answered questions.

What prison?

A prison in the State of New York.

Ahhh!

A man motioned to a red leather couch in the comfortably
furnished room. There were white curtains, a few cages with
birds singing in them, and under my feet a green carpet.
Much light came in at a high window.

A small man entered. He wore a long, tightly buttoned
black coat. One of his hands was in a black glove; he held
this hand in back of him. He had a small white spade beard,
a distinguished face. He stood away about ten feet from me,
and bowed. I got up.

He said, "Sing Sing?" I answered, "Sing Sing." The
door opened again and a young man was shown in. The

little old man turned to him and said with raised eyebrows, "Warden Lawes, Sing Sing."

The Director bowed deeply. He was followed by a retinue of secretaries and assistants and guards. As he sat down on the couch beside me and pumped my hand, he repeated "Sing Sing" as if it were the name of his first love. He picked a stray hair off the collar of my coat, and then, standing up, I was introduced to the staff, and someone was quickly sent for something to drink. An order was given for luncheon, and then from a drawer of his desk the Director slipped a worn Colt .25 into his pocket and said, "Permit me," and went ahead.

"I will go ahead," he said. "You do not know the way."

He was athletic, of good bearing; I think partly Indian. His clothes were simple; he used his chest and lips at times as Mussolini does, the body swaying with both hands at the hips, the lower lip rolled out as in pouting.

We passed two heavy gates, went through a long tunnel, turned to the right, and entered one of the cellblocks in the star-shaped building.

"Our population in this prison is five hundred and five men, and twenty-four women. Most of them are here for crimes of passion. The population of Ecuador is about three million."

"Where does the music come from?"

"From the political prisoners. We have three of them. They are not forced to work, so they sing and play guitars; here they are."

Without stopping their song, the three young men nodded to the Warden. They were in a cell with flowers at the window and a small parrot in a cage; two sat on the bed, the third on a three-legged stool.

"Now we go to the shops." We crossed a wide square and entered a house filled with the noises of hammering, sawing, the smell of wood and leather, and above that the smell of lilies from the prison yard. The prisoners sang here also; the windows were high and without bars. They stood up as the Warden came in; their faces remained at ease. Shoes were made here and some furniture, small trunks lined with paper on which flower designs were printed. In another part of the room men were carving small skulls out of ivory nuts, and one was arranging a miniature of the Crucifixion scene inside a small bottle. Some of the men smoked, some rested, all smiled as the Warden spoke to them. They all very proudly showed their work. The Warden told them all, "Warden Lawes—Sing Sing," and in a few words described my famous prison to them. He stopped and spoke to several men and told me what crimes they had committed. Some of the men asked him questions, and he answered with interest, thinking awhile before he spoke. He usually touched the men or held them by the arm; he bowed and smiled when he had finished with them, and he told his assistant to note several things the men requested.

From this room we climbed the stone steps up to the roof of the prison. Lilies were blooming in the gardens below; on the south side there was a swimming pool into which a stream of water poured from the mouth of a stone lion. A sentry lay on the roof. He got up and kicked the magazine under his pill-box and reached for the rifle which lay on the blanket on which he had been reading; he pulled down his coat and started pacing up and down, the gun over his shoulder.

"Does anyone ever escape from here?"

"Yes, sometimes," said the Warden. "Here, right here, is where they escape." He pointed to the roof of the cellblock that was nearest to the mountain. To clear a wall that is eighteen feet high, a man had to run and then jump out and down a distance of some thirty-four feet; he landed in a thicket of candelabra cacti on the other side of the fence. I asked the Warden how they punished the men when they caught them. "If he jumps well," said the Warden, "he's gone. It's not easy; he must want to be free very badly, and I would not like to risk it, would you? His friends will hide him and we have one less prisoner. If he jumps badly, he falls down into the yard here and is perhaps dead—at least he will break both his legs. He will never jump again; the pain, that is enough punishment. And you, Señor; in Sing Sing, what you do?"

"Oh, we lock them up in a dungeon, with bread and water and no light, for a week, two weeks, a month."

"I do not believe in that," he said with the Mussolini gesture. "I do not believe in vengeance. Look here, down over the edge; this man is a bad fellow, I had to do something. I have put him alone by himself on half-rations. But I gave him the dog and cats and I come to see him and talk to him. I am troubled with his stupidity."

I crept to the edge of the roof and looked down. In a court by himself sat a young, wild-haired fellow. His half-ration consisted of a big bowl of soup, a small pail half full of rice, and a loaf of black bread. The dog and cats were sitting close to him waiting for the remnants of his meal.

"You know," continued the Warden, "he is my only problem prisoner; before, it was full of them. The military ran this institution; the military mind is stupid—boom, huuuump, march, one, two, three, four, eyes right—shouting, marching is all they know. I am an advocate; I try to be humanitarian; not soft, please do not mistake me, I mean economic with life; that is my idea. I look at my prisoner when he comes in, I have studied the science of criminology, I have a knowledge of the system Bertillon. I am sorry when a man is brought in and I can see by his nose, his eyes, his jaw, and his skull, that he is a bad fellow for whom I can do nothing. That one I send away, to the Galápagos. It's not bad for them there; they can sleep and fish. Here he would do terrible damage.

"Here I keep the men and women who have perhaps even killed somebody, who have done something in one moment of their life that was wrong; they know it, I know it, we're both sorry; let us make the best of it. First of all I tell them to forget it and work. I know each man here. I hope they all like me as much as I like them.

"We have no death penalty here in Ecuador. The maximum sentence is for sixteen years; that is for cold murder.

"All prisoners receive wages, the current wages that would be paid if the man worked outside. The wages are divided in three parts. One-third goes to the prison, and by this the institution supports itself; one-third goes to the man for pocket money; and one-third is saved for him, with interest, for the day when he is freed. If he has a family, the pocket money and the savings account are split according to the needs of his wife and children, but he must re-

ceive some money for himself and a small sum for his freedom; he may not want to go back to his family. Any of
them can go out, if I say yes. A prisoner's wife can visit
him; she can go out into the garden with him, and bring
his children. He can sometimes go home with her. And I like
it when they paint. Here, look into this cell."

We had come down from the roof. Almost every cell had
pictures in watercolors or crayons—simple pictures of landscapes, saints, animals, in flat poster effects; some in brilliant colors, some uncertain and shaky. They were painted
on the walls of the cells and sometimes along the corridors.

The Warden knew all the rare ones. He showed them to
me with pride, and particular pride at the absence of por-
nographic ones.

"I would let them alone if there were any," he said. "A
man's cell is his private room here. He can do what he
wants. I am just glad I have never found any.

"Now let us go to the women."

The twenty-four women live in a prison within the
prison. Here there are more flowers, three tangerine trees,
and clouds of linen hanging over them.

These women have stabbed cheating lovers; one of them
did away with her baby. They spend their days washing and ironing the drawers, undershirts, and socks of the
cadets at the military academy. Their children are with
them. Little boys and girls run and sing in the yard. They
go out to school and come back to eat with Mama. The little
houses, of one room each, are orderly, and all the women
were smiling. One was nursing her baby.

"Born here," said the Warden with pride, and pinched
its cheeks.

We said our good-bys and walked back to the reception room. While we waited for luncheon he pouted again in the Mussolini manner, crossed his legs, and looked out of the window over Quito. He turned abruptly to pose a question which apparently had difficulty in forming itself into words.

"Señor Lawes," he blurted, "I have heard so much of you. I have read so much in magazines. Your stories are published in our Spanish journals very often. I have seen a moving picture that you have written. You are such an intelligent man and so—what is the word?—efficient, and also —what is it?—versatile. How you do it? Here I have a little prison with five hundred people. I am busy all day and half the night and every Sunday—I have not had a vacation for a year. How can you do it? I think it's wonderful."

17

Poor Animal. The Arena de Toros in
Quito seats about a thousand people, one leaning out over
the shoulders of another. On Sunday afternoons it fills to
the battered brass music of the municipal band fortified by
the players from a regimental band.

The boxes are cement cubicles which form the base of the
structure. Those on the shady side of the ring are occupied
by Society and the diplomats. From the boxes well-dressed
five- and six-year-olds dangle their legs into a narrow corridor, which provides a haven for the fighters. It receives
them out of the dangers of the ring as they leap with grace,
when time allows, over the wooden balustrade. This protective fence is strong, worn, and splintered. It carries a few
advertisements and is about five and a half feet high. Here
in Quito, the bulls also jump over it and are booed for it.

Bullfighting, I am told, is a very expensive sport. The
local impresarios are not rich enough to endow it properly.
Outside of the opera *Carmen* I know little or nothing of
what a real bullfight should be. I have never read Mr. Hem-
ingway's book on it, nor had I ever seen a fight in Spain or
anywhere else when I went to my first in Quito.

Bullfighting cannot possibly be anything like the vicious,
slow butchery that is performed here.

All over the town are flamboyant posters: in the upper
right corner a lithograph of a giant bull, under it the
portraits of the two fighters, and at the bottom the
heavy-lettered announcement that the "BRAVISSIMOS
TOROS DE ANTISANO"—the most brave bulls of Antisano—will be fought.

I had not seen the bulls, but the fighters live at my hotel; their room is two doors away from mine, they eat a few tables away from me in the dining room. They are men with ordinary faces, hard to classify: not sportsmen, not mugs, not businessmen; perhaps rather the nondescript young man who just works at a grocery, who comes to fix the telephone, or hangs around a billiard academy—the Latin edition of such a young man. They eat hunched over with their faces almost on the plate, they drink with moderation. One of them stares at a full-bosomed woman during most of his meals. They seem without bravado, and here in the hotel no one pays any attention to them.

On Sunday, they don't appear for luncheon. About two in the afternoon they come into the lobby, clad in tight, gold-embroidered costumes, one white, the other a patched, faded old rose. Then they wait in front of the hotel and a friend drives up in an old Lincoln touring car with the top down. The porter places the two embossed sword cases and the capes on the front seat next to the driver. The fighters climb in, their pants almost splitting as they bend over; seated, they wave their hands at a small group of admirers. Little boys hang on the door handles and ride on the running board. They drive off to the arena.

Marching into the ring, they have grown in stature: the music, the bright sunlight on the yellow sand, the ritual, and the cheering crowd lend them height and power.

The municipal band fills the arena with a tune from a Fred Astaire film; it's the song, "Dancing Cheek to Cheek." They play this over and over. I don't know the proper names for the entire retinue, but they all disappear in the shelter of the wooden balustrade. A bolt is taken from a heavy door, it opens, and out of its shadow trots the bull. Black, lithe, alert, he dances almost to the center, head held high, then he reaches for the spike that has been stuck into his side under a blue rosette. He licks at it with his tongue.

The bull is the son of little cattle. The high altitude is given as reason for his smallness, and also for the absence of horses.

The game starts. It is interrupted by trumpet signals, by changes in formation and various ceremonials. The animal charges sometimes, and there are brief moments when he angrily passes close to a man and comes out from under the cape in bewildered surprise. Salvos of applause greet the fighter's turns in these maneuvers, his form, his timing. This goes on and on; the animal is winded and stops for air, his tongue out, like a panting dog.

Not until after the banderillas are stuck into him does the little bull sense the purpose of his presence. It is then that he loses his water, that he soils his hind legs and trembles. He looks around for help—at the closed door through which he came, at the wide ring of faces, and at the one means of escape, over which he has chased several of his tormentors—the wooden ring. He runs, clears it with his front legs, and awkwardly clambers over, pulling his hind legs after him.

It is at this part of the performance that shock and disgust begin. It would seem as if at this point, in the name of sport, or simply because of a dull performance, the animal should be dismissed. He has shown that he is scared, that he does not choose to fight, that he has mistaken the whole thing for play in the fields. The time allowed for his killing has already been stretched to the limit and beyond. But he remains.

The crowd boos. The torero is in the center of the ring. He raises both shoulders and tilts his head in the gesture of "What can I do with such a bull?" He walks over to the partition, his sword in his right hand, and stabs it into the animal's haunches to drive him to an opening twenty feet ahead which leads back into the arena. The animal cannot turn. Its back, torn by the banderilla harpoon ends, is a dripping shawl of dark blood. The long rods above his shoulders sway and tear his wounds at every motion. The little boys reach down to twist the banderillas out of him to take home as souvenirs.

To make him go back, the torero and his crew keep stabbing harder, cursing louder. Step by step they succeed.

Slowly the bull steps out into the arena. He sways, he is weak, blood rains from him. The fighter confronts him with a gesture that might be beautiful and exciting, if it were opposite an angered, dangerous, and fearless animal. He measures along his sword, whips up on his toes, levers his body over the sunken head of the animal, high between the horns, and—to the applause of the whole audience—rams the blade into the shoulders of the bull. He misses his aim; he has stuck the sword into bone.

A mute, distant moan comes from the animal. It is a sickening sound and a sickening picture. The sword shakes. With pitiful, inadequate despair the little bull charges his attacker. The torero disappears behind the fence; two other men dance in with capes and turn the animal from him.

This gory act repeats itself until three swords are stuck into the bull, not one of them having found its target.

The bull is in a small quarter-moon-shaped strip of afternoon shadow. There he sinks onto his knees, close to the door which he hoped would open for him. It does, and out of it comes the only mercy of that afternoon, a man in a red shirt with a short dagger. He ends the disgrace with two quick stabs behind the animal's head.

This is a reconciling thing, relief, and quite the nicest part. With an acquiescent nod, like a child falling asleep, the animal turns its head and sinks down on its knees, quite naturally, as in prayer. A chain is put around the horns and three horses drag the limp body out, scraping a wide path across the arena.

The band plays "Dancing Cheek to Cheek" once more; the torero drinks a glass of water, to be refreshed for the next bull. Everybody is applauding him; no one is leaving.

18

The Promised Land. "The green

hut in which we lived stood in a lagoon of turquoise water.
To the left and right of it soared high curtains of greenery,
and between these and beyond a beach of coral sand was the
sky, liquid, yellow as chartreuse in a thin glass.

"The sun came up and birds spread their wings and sank
down to the lagoon. Flamingos made pink question marks
with their necks and then searched the water for sardines
and small frogs.

"Down out of the high bamboo structure of the roof,
where he sat motionless and hunted flies and mosquitoes all
night, climbed Tala, the pet chameleon. He changed to the
color of the sky, to the blue of the water. As Waha's soft,
small hands caressed him, he made short flute-like sounds
and the comb on his head began to glow, first like the dying
fire in an iron stove, then more intensely like a fiery lance;
and on his body's sides, on the gills, and in the soft, loose
folds of skin under his throat appeared brilliant orange
flames.

"A barbaric ornament, he sat on the girl's shoulder, and
the two points of the blood-red whip of his tongue danced
into her hair, to her neck, and shot through her slender
fingers.

"No woman's body on the whole island was softer. Of
the three women that Womo, the Headman of Tago Tago,
had given me, she was the tallest and so young that her
teeth had not been filed. A wreath of camellias went from
her shoulders to her abdomen, the largest and most beautiful of the flowers lay over the softly pulsating groove be-

tween her firm bosoms. She folded the mat on which we had slept. A small red bug was hidden under the mat. She crushed it between her white teeth and with the red liquid painted the eyes of a faded turtle carved into the side of the hut. I had obtained all this, together with an outrigger canoe and several miles of beach, from the chief, in return for an umbrella, an old opera hat, and a pair of spectacles without lenses. . . ."

This Gauguin idyl was the opening effusion of a serial of 50,000 labored words, my first exercise in fiction on a typewriter, composed before I had ever seen a palm tree outside of a hotel. It was written mostly at night, many years ago, and sent by registered mail to the *Ladies' Home Journal*. It came back with the magazine's editorial regrets. I have put it away in my trunk, the trunk in which publishers find unpublished manuscripts shortly after the author dies. It is up in the attic, where this trunk is always discovered. The beach in Tago Tago, the hut, and the sunrise remained a blue dream tent in which I sat for a few years; and I forgot all about it until I came to Ecuador. For those who still dream, the jungles, the seacoast, the tropic isles, and the mountains of Ecuador offer all the scenery, every variety of climate, and they are the ideal proving ground for adventure and escape; but the dreams seldom seem to come true, and the people who are happy here would also be happy in Scranton or Tallahassee. There are spectacular failures, mild, resigned ends, and unhappy finales in fever or return home—and there are also compromises in the form of jobs as sewing-machine salesmen or as agents for condensed-milk companies and Crisco.

The two outstanding examples of yes and no that I met

in Ecuador are André Roosevelt and a retired German
major of infantry who was an amateur zoologist. Neither
has chosen to live in as unbuttoned a paradise as I imagined
on the beach of Tago Tago. Both are married, have a complete wardrobe, live with their lawfully wedded wives, and
even brought their dogs along.

The German major has a place along the River Pastaza.
His house is a neat mountain chalet with window boxes and
a small brass plate on the door, with the major's name and
title neatly engraved on it. Next to the name plate, and the
only one in the jungle, is a doorbell. Underneath is a scraper
for dirty boots, and inside is a mat with *"Willkommen"*
written on it.

The property stands in overwhelming scenery, with
mountains all around it, and faces the long silver ribbon
of a waterfall. Monkeys fly from limb to limb of tall trees,
parrots chatter everywhere. One of them is domesticated;
it walks around and speaks German and Spanish. *"Gott im
Himmel,"* he says, and *"Guten Tag,"* *"Buenos días"* and
"Mamacita." In the garden along sanded walks that are
neatly raked stand benches made of lignum vitae. There is
a tame tapir, an animal half-pig, half-elephant; and a very
serious and ancient Galápagos turtle feeds on cacti. The
turtle is the color of rock; his eyes are dull, and he stands
on heavy legs like those of a rhino and crunches thorny cac-
tus leaves as a cow chews grass. There is an egret that follows the major like a dog, and there are two dogs, Great
Danes, that lie under huge avocado trees. The dogs' eyes
are on the foliage above, their heads lie between outstretched paws, and when they hear the rustling of leaves
or the sound of a breaking twig they come to attention and

bump into each other trying to catch the pears that fall
from the trees. They carry the fruit to a corner of the patio,
and with their lips drawn back from the teeth they gnaw
away the soapy skin, eat the meat, and then play with the
stone until the major's wife comes out of the kitchen and
tells them to stop and get out of her garden, where German
vegetables grow in orderly rows: kohlrabi, soup greens,
black radishes, root celery, and red cabbages.

Major Timmel sat with me under an arbor that rained its
sweet blossoms over tables and chairs and into the soft wind
that carried them across to the house. We had walked to the
waterfall and visited the cages in which he kept various animals and birds. The major had brought back several orchids of immoral design, astounding flowers, like hats in-
vented by a lewd modiste. He held one of them in his hand,
and as he spoke dismembered it carelessly, dropping the
petals down into the soft sand. He sighed, "*Ja—Frühling
giebt es für mich nur in Deutschland.*" Spring, the month
of May, existed for him only in Germany. He spoke of the
beauty of pine trees in winter, of the gurgling of melted
water running under the snow, of the first crocuses, of the
unfolding of the horse chestnut's leaves and of its blossoms,
of thaw and violets, and of a little geranium carefully
nursed through the winter in a red clay pot on a window.
Outside the window, a cobbled tidy street, small houses on
both sides, little women going to church. "Do you know
anyone—who would buy this godforsaken place?

"I have installed electric light, all sanitary conveniences.
I have forty devoted Indians who work my land. I plant
sugar, cacao, coffee. I hunt and fish. There are no taxes, no
interference from the Government. The sun rises at six and

sets at six every day. In back of my house is a natural pool with hot, healing water that is excellent to drink when you cool it—it tastes like Vichy. My wife came here with arthritis—couldn't move a finger. Now she's completely cured.

"The Government is most generous: you get free three times as much land as you cultivate—a marvelous opportunity for a young man. I will sell for anything and go back to Pomerania," he said, with a sweeping gesture. The major's wife served coffee, knitted with the arthritic hands, and sat in silence, only occasionally nodding in agreement when he spoke.

As everyone does here, the major attached himself immediately to me with all his hopes, fears, and troubles. They poured out of him in an unhalting stream. He showed me books and photographs, explained his circumstances and, with an air of the greatest confidence, he began to speak of Franklin Delano Roosevelt.

"I have no use for a man who almost always smiles; I am suspicious of that sort of humor." He leaned closer and said, "Neutrality—ha—hahaha!" The parrot echoed the laugh and added, *"Gott im Himmel."*

"Wait a minute," said the major. He disappeared into the house, with the egret at his heels, and came back with two folios, made out of wrapping paper and stitched together. He explained to me that a friend in the States mailed him the *New York Herald Tribune* regularly, and that since even before the beginning of the war he had clipped all items relating to Germany out of the *Tribune* and pasted them into the two books. In one he pasted the good, in the other the bad—one book was thick and the other thin. In the thick one were essays by Miss Thompson, underlined in part with red ink, and accompanied on the margins with exclamation marks and the words, "Lies, lies, nothing but lies," also in red ink. The other volume was thin and its pages blank except for a statement from Poultney Bigelow, a speech of Charles Lindbergh's, and a report of the Quakers' committee from their Berlin correspondent.

He showed me next, in the bad book, a picture of the Sixth Avenue elevated railroad being torn down, and explained to me that this was one of Roosevelt's undertakings to help the Allies. The elevated railroad, he told me, was shipped directly to Liverpool, to be made into munitions. He had heard this in a German broadcast, and now, he informed me, Roosevelt was busy trying to tear down also the Ninth, the Third, and the Second and First Avenue elevateds, also to send to the Allies. No, he did not like, he said once more, a man who always smiled.

When I rode back to town, his wife gave me some sausage and cheese and a bottle of good coffee to take along. He rode with me a good distance and outlined the future. He told me what would become of India, of the Dutch East Indies, and of England. He left me when we came to a swinging bridge and shouted that he hoped I would find someone to buy his place; now that Germany would become a fit land to live in again, he wanted to return, he shouted, across the turbulent water.

André Roosevelt has always found it easy to live in tropical places. He spent years in Bali and is now happy in Ecuador. Half an hour out of Quito at the foot of Mount Pichincha is his small house in a large garden.

The reason I think that André Roosevelt is happy here

THE HOUSE AND GARDEN OF ANDRÉ ROOSEVELT IN QUITO

is that he has taken with him most of the troubles of civilization; with less pressure, and much less hurry and noise,
he has access to our griefs: visits from unpleasant people,
bills to pay, disputes with tradesmen, overdrawn bank
accounts, callers from the telephone company, Christmas
shopping, plumbing out of order, and doctor, lawyer, dentist; and for Ruth, his wife, there are hats and dresses,
either to envy or to laugh at. There are also the many
cares of running a house, which is no more exempt than
one in Scarsdale from the need of being painted, and the
large garden that must be kept in order. . . .

"Look at my garden. Ruth planted these forget-me-nots
only last week, and now look at them." The flowers, innocently blue as the cloak of the Virgin of Quinché, are up to
children's elbows; the daisies are as big as the faces of
alarm clocks; the garden hums with colibri, bright and expensive as a Cartier window.

The garden sings, the bushes say good-morning to you
as you walk past them. It is not out of a René Clair scenario
but a sensible garden: the voices come from the children of
the servants who stand among bushes, plucking dead leaves,
loosening earth, watering flowers. *"Buenos días, patrón,"*
they sing, and, *"Buenos días, patroncita."* Two of them
belong to the cook, others to the gardener, the most beautiful to Cirilio, the butler.

This Cirilio at first meeting is a fearful man. He is as
wide as he is high. His thick black hair grows from his eyebrows back down to his shoulder-blades. He can pick up
things from the floor without bending, and André Roosevelt says that he spends the night sitting in a tree. The children's dresses are made of old Roosevelt curtains and Ciri

lio's wardrobe also comes from his master. His wife cuts
the pants off in the middle; then she takes the two lower
parts and sews them together, and a few buttons make them
into a second pair of trousers.

The economics of the Roosevelt ménage are very simple.
A hundred dollars a month covers all expenses, including
rent, auto hire, entertaining, and the salaries and food for
the servants and their children's food. Cirilio gets $2.50 a
month; and the cooks get $2.00 each. The cooks are not
very good in Ecuador, but then you have two of them.

Roosevelt has two cooks. One day we shot a rabbit up
near the summit of Mount Pichincha and brought it home.
The cooks had never cooked a rabbit before, and with
Indian patience they sat for hours by the side of the duck
pond and plucked the rabbit.

Ruth Roosevelt takes the fashion magazine to which she
subscribes to a tailor in Quito, buys cloth which the Indians
weave and dye, and is well dressed.

There is some difficulty with servants. All the servants
are Indians. They are very sensitive, easily offended. They
usually leave in the middle of a dinner party. When they
are scolded for something they become sad, take their
gloves off, and go home to their mountains and sit under
a tree and eat bananas for a few days. Unannounced, and
without explanation, they return, kiss your hand, and say
that they have missed you.

Cirilio is more than sensitive. He must never be repri-
manded when he forgets anything. If André says to him,
"Cirilio, you must remember not to serve on the right side
of the guests, but on the left," the damage is done. The
reflection of the candles in his large black eyes becomes

hazy, he puts the dish down, beats himself on the chest, and makes a long speech. "Oh, I am so stupid!" he starts out. "I have the head of a cow—on the right—no, on the left. Oh, you have told me so often, patrón!" Nothing can stop him. The food gets cold and Cirilio is gone to the hills with his children, insulting himself all the way.

When all goes well, he is happy and sings, and he is very much attached to the patroncita. He follows her throughout the house with paintpots, brushes, canvas gloves, and a ladder. Ruth loves to paint. The house always smells of fresh paint, mostly a terrible shade of blue. In overalls, brushing her blond hair out of her face with her forearm, she paints floors, garden furniture, tables, benches, doors, and window shutters. Cirilio holds the ladder and points to corners that have been forgotten, and apologizes. He knows that the patroncita likes to have everything painted new. That is one of the few things he is certain about.

To give a party is a nervous, dangerous obligation in Quito, largely on account of the servant problem. André gave a cocktail party. We went to Quito to buy wine and whisky and food. Spirits and imported wines—champagnes and brandy—are the only expensive items for entertaining in Ecuador. We were returning loaded with packages when André saw some pâté de foie gras in the window of a small shop. He is very fond of pâté de foie gras, and we bought all the cans the man had. They were dusty, and the proprietor of the shop blew on them and wiped them off with his sleeve.

After we came home and started a white wine punch, André got a box of crackers and we went out to the garden to a newly painted table and benches with the six cans of pâté de foie gras. Each of them sucked in air with a "Fhhh-ssss" as it was opened. The pâté had shriveled up. It seemed very old and looked like chewing gum. André moved away from the cans and smeared the pâté on the crackers at arm's length, and he said nothing. But there was a tin of anchovies, and he put on each cracker two filets of anchovies, laying them crisscross on top of the pâté. There was also a tube of some very sharp-tasting paste, and out of this tube André squeezed a rosette, just in the center where the anchovies crossed. We finally stuck a stuffed olive on the whole business. We made about forty of these canapés, and when they were done, Mr. Roosevelt took one and ate it. "Much better," he said, and handed one to me. "In fact, it tastes damn good. Have one." It was terrible.

André went to dress. He goes about most of the day in a long robe, a vegetable-dyed purple piece of hair cloth designed by his wife. Cirilio lit the candles, straightened out the silver, buttoned his white jacket, and was constantly asking the patroncita if he was doing everything right. The patroncita went to dress, and then all at once Cirilio disappeared. He had remembered that the patroncita loved to have everything painted fresh.

When the first guests arrived, Cirilio was standing alone in the lobby, his kind eyes shining. He passed the tray of canapés to them, but they could not take them. They held their hands far away from themselves. The hands were blue. Cirilio had just painted the doors, the doorknobs, the railings. "Oh, I am the head of a cow!" he said, when he saw what had happened—and then he was gone, and he did not come back for a long time.

19

Buenos Días, Gran Hotel.

The train from Quito down to Esmeraldas on the northern coast is somewhat smaller than the one that comes up from Guayaquil, and it does not go to Esmeraldas, but that is planned. The engine and the coaches are already marked "Ferrocarril Quito–Esmeraldas."

There are three coaches, the first for baggage, the second for Indians. This one is insufficient, and most of the Indian passengers, together with their chickens, sit on the roof. Occasionally they bring one of their saints along, a statue decked out with flowers, and then it becomes a gay train, filled with color and music—it looks like a gondola coming down the Grand Canal. The third car is divided into two parts; the half that is toward the Indians is plain first class, the end toward the landscape is the observation car.

In this last part are six wicker chairs, upholstered in a stout, faded kind of billiard cloth. On the seats are rings such as the bottoms of wet beer glasses leave on a table. They come from the steel springs that have wormed their way up through the horsehair. You sit on them unless you have brought a pillow along or a blanket.

But you have ample chance to change your mind about the ride. From the moment you arrive at the depot until the train leaves you are surrounded by chauffeurs who plead with you to let them drive you to Otavalo, the last station. It's more comfortable, faster, and it won't cost much more, they tell you. As train time approaches, their advice becomes anguished. They run after you and take hold of your arm. "Don't take the train, go by car." They pull the corners of their mouths down and point at the engine, the train, or the conductor. "Don't go! Don't take it! It's terrible!" They say this under the nose of the station-master.

It is seven-thirty by the sun, a quarter to seven by the bells on the cathedral, and ten minutes to seven by the station clock. (There is an observatory in Quito which has the right time, but it cannot be seen from here.) The train leaves at seven sharp; that is, when the station-master whistles and the engineer waves good-by to him.

As you pull away, you see the city first below you, then above. You ride through a wild garden without fences. Everywhere grow white lilies, geranium trees stand in all the gardens, costly birds fly through the air, and in the early hours when the clouds hang low in the valleys the landscape is as clear and luminous as if it were painted on the side of a very thin porcelain cup. It is, moreover, neat in its wildness; all the leaves, the plants, and the grass are washed and combed. Wherever you look, it is a picture out of the Bible, and the sparrows have little combs on their heads, like small roosters. I believe this is the most beautiful and the most varied landscape I have seen in all my life.

On several sharp curves the conductor will point out to you places where the engine has jumped the track and rolled over. The engineer and the fireman jumped to safety. They were going too fast, explains the conductor. Midway between Quito and Otavalo, he comes and offers you a tray with dusty sandwiches and lukewarm beer.

The train stops at a small village about every half-hour. The village surrounds it—small earthen houses with walls on which cubaya plants grow, little black boars, Indian children who ride on the train out of the village while the conductor stays behind and embraces a friend. When the train is already under way, the conductor runs after it, and swings himself to the rear platform. He smiles. Everyone smiles. This is really new, all of it.

Sometime during the journey the conductor comes with a little board to which is attached a paper. He has a pencil stub which he wets with his lips; then he asks you for your name, nationality, and profession, where you are going, where you come from, and why. You can give him any answer you choose. He writes it down politely in the letters of a six-year-old. If you are asleep, he waits. He whispers the questions to you if anyone else is asleep in the car. If you are a political menace, then, a rebel, a fugitive, or an assassin, just stay asleep until you reach your destination. No one will know that you have left Quito for Ibarra, Tulcán, or Alaosi.

On the day I went to Otavalo a man sat opposite me, asleep. At a sudden stop for water he woke up, unpacked some food, offered me half of it, and then started a conversation. "Madame Alvarez and I have wanted to be a father for many years," he said. "We have tried everything to be a father, Madame Alvarez and I, for about sixteen years, ever since we were married. But it is of no consequence; we are not a father. Madame Alvarez has even burned candles to her saint, all for nothing.

"Then, one time, Madame Alvarez goes to visit a sister in Chile, for one months"—he held up his right index finger and repeated—"for one months." The finger again—"In one months, Señor, I am a father. That is why I am on this train, I am visiting my niño, I am visiting as a father once a month. And you, señor?"

"I am also visiting a niño. I am writing a children's book, and I am looking for a child, an Indian child, to find out how he lives and what he looks like."

He then gave me the name and address of the schoolmaster in Otavalo, and offered to take me to a good hotel there, and he told me that he also had been a literary man, a publisher in Santiago, Chile.

He scratched the outside of one fat hand with the fingers of the other and then told me that his paper had failed because it was an afternoon paper.

"My paper had a small circulation, about twelve thousand. That is not enough. The circulation was so bad, my friend, because it was an afternoon paper. We have an alcoholic problem down there. Everybody drinks, and at five o'clock when my paper comes out nobody cares about anything, nobody can read any more. We have tried to print it in very large, easily readable type, but the same results. Now I have a small hotel in Quito."

The train dipped down into a valley that looked like the badlands of North Dakota. The Indians sang on the roof of the train and my companion began to snore. When he woke again he peeled a banana, and as the conductor passed and held out his hand for the ticket, he gave him the banana peel. The conductor took it and opened the door to throw it out. Then the brakes screeched and we were in Otavalo.

Otavalo is like all other mountain cities—marketplace with cathedral and Government house, municipal band, Indians in white clothes and ponchos, more beautiful than any other Indians; donkeys everywhere, and a large shop filled with coffins. (The death rate, the infant mortality, is appalling here. The little coffins are like cigar boxes, unpainted, and cost thirty cents apiece.)

Before Señor Alvarez went to visit his niño he took me to the principal of the school, Señor Andrade. This earnest man lived in one room and a kitchen. Every object in the room wore a little black necktie: four such cravats were tied on the four feet of the couch, one black bow across each picture on the wall, one across the neck of the Virgin, one on each cooking pot, and one across a small statue of Harlequin and Columbine. The teacher explained to me that six months ago his wife had died in childbirth, that she had been fond of all these things and had held them in her lovely hands, and that they were in mourning for her. He put on a black hat and we went to his school. The school was large, with light rooms. There was a basketball net in the yard.

The teacher told me that the Ministry of Education was very advanced in its ideas and that as soon as it was at all possible they instructed children in the matter of sex. He waved to his honor pupil, a little boy, and asked him to bring his homework. He handed me a homemade blank book. Just as our children at that age make their first designs of houses and people, here there was a picture in colors, and very modernistic, of a man in profile with "El Estómago" written under it. The man seemed to have just eaten; the estómago was filled with small pencil dots. The next page showed teeth and the digestive system, and then came a page on which the title was decorated like a Christmas card, with sunrays, little stars, scrolls, and illumination surrounding the words "La Sífilis." Equally beautiful and fetching was the next title, "La Gonorrea." This was done in green, with darts. The teacher explained that such instruction prevents shock later on.

We went back to my hotel, the Hotel Sucre. The waiter's name was Francisco. He was an Indian and barefooted, and he was also the cook. Francisco also helps clean the rooms and water the lilies. The hotel has one story and is square. The seven rooms face out on the courtyard. The rooms have no windows—the door is left open. The food is terrible and very cheap. You eat out in the courtyard. It is one of the most beautiful hotels I have ever been in. Francisco, walking silently, is always near; you can't complain about the service.

As I ate some boiled eggs, a man came out of room No. 4 and introduced himself. He was the chancellor of the Belgian Legation in Quito. His car had broken down and he was waiting for it to be fixed.

He held his head and said, "Have you ever seen anything like the hotels in this country? Oooooooh! I don't mind this one so much, but in Guayaquil, the first day I arrive, I say, 'Portez-moi un journal.'

"The telephone answers, 'Good, Señor.'

"Half an hour later I telephone again, and as the paper has not arrived, I say once more, 'Send me a paper.' Half an hour later a boy arrives and asks me what I want. 'A paper, where is the paper? The paper that I asked for half an hour and an hour ago, where is it?'

"He answers me nothing.

" 'Ah,' I said, 'that means you have no confidence in me. You want to have the money first, the twenty centavos!'

" 'Oh, no, patrón,' he said. 'That is not so.'

"But he held out his hand. I gave him the twenty centavos and he brought the paper.

"A few days later on, I find outside my neighbor's door a paper on which is written 'Buenos días, Gran Hotel.'

"I call the boy. I show him the paper. I say to him, 'What does that mean?'

"He says, 'It means, "Bon jour, Grand Hotel. Good day, Grand Hotel." '

"I said to him, 'Don't take me for an idiot! I know what it means, Buenos días, Gran Hotel.'

"And I said once more, 'Why is "Buenos días, Gran Hotel" written on this paper?' And he answered, the stupid, 'It is written there because it is the paper which is brought to the guests.'

"I said, 'Why don't you write "Buenos días, Gran Hotel" on the paper you bring for me?'

"To that he had no answer. And then I said, 'Good, I will give you the explanation. You are, all of you, *une bande de dégoûtants*. I know very well that the papers with "Buenos días, Gran Hotel" are offered to the clients with the compliments of the hotel, and only because I occupy the most expensive suite here and because I am a foreigner, you take me for a fool and make me pay. That is why; now go.'

"Cher Bemelmans," he said, "write that in your journal."

I asked Francisco, who had listened to all this with big Indian eyes, standing in the shadow of the door, for pen and ink, and then I wrote it down word for word as he had said it. Francisco stood in back of me and read over my shoulder. When I had finished, as the ink was wet, he took some earth from the wall of the hotel, rubbed it to dust between his hands, and shook it over the paper to dry the ink.

The wine was rancid here. The proprietor brought his horse in from the street, a white horse, and it lay down in the center of the courtyard among the lilies. Francisco washed a shirt and hung it between the pillars that held up the roof. The moon rose, and a bird came and sang in the courtyard. The lilies and the white horse drank up the light. Francisco brought a lamp into my room, and then he looked through my trunk, examined the camera, looked through pictures, took the razor apart, and asked what was in the bottle. He sprinkled the eau de cologne on his head and asked me what the Belgian had said about "Buenos días, Gran Hotel."

He raked his thick black hair with my comb; then he became sleepy. The bed was large—boards and the usual beaten old mattress. He fell asleep at the foot of it, and I covered him up. He was about ten years old.

The next morning he brought me a newspaper. It was old and had lain in the hotel for about a month, but on it he had written in crude letters, "Buenos días, Gran Hotel."

20

The Painted Grapes. The pro-

prietor was snoring in his room, and the beds creaked in
the rooms of all the guests whenever they turned in their
sleep. I lay for a long while with my arms crossed in back
of my head and watched the sunrise through the open door.
There was no window in my room. None of the rooms of
this hotel has windows. The doors all face the courtyard.

The donkeys sang in the mountains outside, and in the
room next to mine I heard the noises of a man getting up.
He poured water into a basin, walked in slippers across the
floor, stropped his razor, and yawned. A Saint Bernard dog
with matted fur and feet as big as a lion's, his face unhappy
and great loose bags under his hopeless, bloodshot eyes,
walked out into the patio and rubbed his pelt against the
wooden column.

His master, in a nightshirt, a glass of water and a tooth-
brush in hand, came after him. The man looked up into the
sky, scratched himself, and then gargled and brushed his
teeth and spat the water into the gutter of the patio. He
then bent over the plot of lilies, smelled them, and disappeared again in his room, where I heard him sit down on
the bed.

In the frame of the green door the picture that I had
watched for two hours was again undisturbed: a few feet
away, between the legs of a metal washstand, two lilies and
a few cobblestones, and on the wall across the yard a free
chalk-colored fresco showing a stag hunted by hounds.
Over the picture hung a piece of old roofing with grass
growing between faded tiles and above these tiles far away

was the volcano Tunguragua. It looked like a cone made of ground coffee; an hour ago, before the sun rose, it was indigo, then for a little while it was the color of an eggplant.

Attached to the door that led from the street into the hotel was one of the bells whose lament is heard when one walks into a small shop in France. It clanged at about seven.

Two barefooted Indians and a small black boar came in. Silently, but for the tinkle of three silver Maltese crosses that hung from the woman's shoulder, they sat down, and the man helped his wife to take a baby from her back. She reached up into her hat and took clean linen from it and changed the baby's clothes. They then sat down under the painting of the stag and the hounds, and the small boar rooted in the soil among the lilies.

The Indians of Otavalo own their land and their houses; they work the ground with wooden plows, raise animals, and bring produce to market. Some of them weave cloth, others are potters. Their linen is spotless. They walk, sit, and stand with exquisite grace.

The men wear black pigtails; they have historic, decided faces, and the women look like the patronesses at a very elegant ball. It is baffling that they achieve this effect just sitting in rows along the sidewalk, their bare feet in the gutter.

The Indian who sat under the deer became impatient; he got up and walked into a room which had one wall lined with rows of bottles of Mallorca and chicha. He helped himself to a bottle and sat down. The two smiled.

The Indians always seem sweet to one another. They talk quietly, and they have a sage arrangement—only one of them, either the husband or the wife, may drink. They take turns. The sober one sees to it that the other gets

INDIANS IN THE PATIO OF THE HOTEL SUCRE IN OTAVALO

home safely. You meet them on all the roads that lead to
Otavalo, their fine faces beaming with majestic friendship.
The children run alongside, everybody sings, a man leads a
woman, a woman pulls a man, no anger, much laughing and
the music of an instrument. They greet you with a sweep of
the beautiful five-pound hat that almost throws them off
the road. They seem a fortunate and happy people.

The Indian in front of me put the bottle away and then
Señor Pilar, the proprietor, came out of his room and
bought the black pig between the spokes at the foot of my
bed, and in the same frame the money changed hands.

The distant volcano Tunguragua was alone again, its
color much lighter now. The sun was half-way up its side.
A coronet of white clouds was near the summit, and at its
base were two rows of eucalyptus trees. From here they
looked like miniature poplars leading up to a château. Between them red spots, the ponchos of Indians far away and
high up, crawled down and disappeared among the blades
of grass on the roof in front of me.

The man next door came again, now in a pair of badly
cut dark gray breeches, not riding breeches and not plus-
fours, but a style half-way between. With these he wore
green woolen golf stockings and high laced black boots.
While he was tying a knot in his cravat a butterfly went
past his face and he ran after it and tried to catch it on
the rim of one of the lilies. The butterfly sailed away and
came through the green doorway into my room, with the
man after it. He caught it, excused himself, and took it to
his room.

After a while he came back and explained to me that the
butterfly was an extraordinary specimen, and, excusing

himself again, he stepped on the foot of my bed, reached to
the ceiling, and collected two cocoons and a large moth.
He delivered a brief lecture on these discoveries, and then
introduced himself as a native of Switzerland, Herr Vogeli,
from Tribschen, on the Vierwaldstättersee, Lake Lucerne.

The dog had come into the room also, and Herr Vogeli
told me how glad he was that he had brought the animal
along to Ecuador. It was, he said, the only good thing that
had happened to him. The dog was of great help; he made
things very comfortable. Whenever they came to stay at a
hacienda or a hotel, he locked the dog into his room for an
hour before retiring. The Saint Bernard acted like a mag-
net. From all the cracks in the floor and the walls, from
closets and out of beds and carpets he drew the hungry
fleas. After an hour he was taken out, doused with a shower
of "la loción Flit," and then Herr Vogeli retired in peace.

He patted his faithful friend. The dog was busy scratch-
ing himself. He tried to reach a spot in back of his ear, lost
his balance, rolled on his side, and violently clicked his teeth
on some evasive fleas in the hair at the tip of his tail.

On the evening of the same day I sat down on a bench in
the Plaza Sucre. A beggar passed first, carrying his old
mother on his back. She held a fan of lottery tickets in her
hand, waved her withered arms, and called, "Twenty thousand sucres next Sunday."

When these two were gone, a group of little people appeared, cretins, Mongoloid children, idiots in a group,
guarded and led by an old man in a wide Panama hat and
a blue linen coat. They huddled together in the camaraderie
of infirmity, their large heads lolling, their limbs in gro-
tesque poses. They bent down over the street with garden

tools, and removed the grass and small plants that grew between the stones. With great effort, they brought the bouquets of weeds to their guardian, who opened a large sack into which they slowly deposited them—watching the old man's face for approval, a smile and nod of the head with which he receipted for the grasses.

From the sack they hopped back to search for more. They laughed, slyly, inwardly, as if in possession of a great and happy secret. They wandered slowly around the plaza. Before the door of the cathedral they knelt down, removed their caps, lifted their faces, and made the sign of the cross.

They looked again for the old man's approval, and went back to the grass, and moved on with their silent smiles, disappearing into the City Hall. There they have a room for their belongings, and another with two rows of small institutional beds, and a large one for the overseer, who is with them day and night.

Outside of the public building stands the Jefe Político, the foreman of a group of citizens whose principle purpose is to keep themselves warm under their ponchos. They stand staring into the square, and, like the cathedral, they are part of every South American plaza. The sight of a young woman, of a cockfight, or of a good horse awakens them and makes them turn their heads. For the rest they stand or sit and gossip. Occasionally one raises an arm to push a necktie to the left or right. He reaches with two fingers into the folds of his skin for a flea. This done, he sinks back into his stupor. If he is a policeman, he blows a little short whistle every half-hour to announce that he is still there.

From the far end of the plaza, between two palm trees, appeared the Swiss, with a cigar box under his arm and followed by his dog. In the box he had new butterflies and cocoons, safely bedded in cotton. The big dog tried to make himself small enough to squeeze under the bench, and his master sat down above him.

With a hand that smelled of ether, Herr Vogeli pointed at the lampposts which stood on the four corners of the plaza and said that exactly at six-twenty the night before he had observed a group of butterflies that appeared from the direction of the volcano. They were all gone in another ten minutes, after flying from lamppost to lamppost. He told me that if he could measure the degree of humidity, then he could make a graph and tell precisely when the butterflies would be here again.

Herr Vogeli seemed to know a good deal about butterflies and insects. I told him how surprising it was to meet a Swiss who was not an innkeeper or the proprietor of a sanatorium.

He said he was very sorry, but that butterflies were only his hobby. He really was a hotelman, and while keeping his eyes on the lampposts, he made me acquainted with his story.

"I am here," he began, "on account of that swine Goldoni. Goldoni is a man who is building a railroad through the jungle down to Esmeraldas. He has been working on it for four years, and in all this time he has finished exactly eight kilometers. He is under arrest now, but that is all beside the point. I came here to open a hotel in Ibarra, a few miles from here, in back of the volcano."

The lamps were lit, there were fluttering wings about them, and Herr Vogeli in his bicycle pants, with the straps sticking out in back of his boots, ran quickly off. He came back, disappointed; the butterflies had not arrived yet, he had found nothing but fairly common moths.

This man Goldoni, he said, sitting down, came to Vogeli's inn one day in Tribschen on the Vierwaldstättersee. It was on that part of this complicated lake that Richard Wagner composed the music for the *Meistersinger* and most of *Siegfried* and *Götterdämmerung*, the place where he spent the happiest years with Frau Cosima—a hallowed spot. A garden restaurant with iron chairs and tables under shade trees reflected itself in the lake. On sunny days it filled up with guests, and above them was the top of the Rigi; it was lovely and peaceful.

When Goldoni came, the garden, the inn, the chairs and tables were dripping; the season was ruined by a month of rain. Vogeli had trouble with his employees, with his wife, and with the three guests who were staying at the inn. They complained about the steam heat being out of order. Goldoni listened to Vogeli's troubles, and then suddenly slapped him on the back and said, "Vogeli, you are my man. Vogeli, you come with me."

He took Vogeli along to the Kursaal in Lucerne, and sat him behind a glass of wine; he pushed the vase of flowers that stood between them out of the way, and while an Italian orchestra played, he told him about Ibarra, about Ecuador.

"Ha," laughed Goldoni, "imagine a land where every vegetable and flower grows wild, where you can get all the help for ten francs a month, and where there is no such thing as a strike or rain." (It rained a little, he said, but only during the night.) Ecuador, the Land of the Future,

where it is spring the year round. In the most beautiful part
of that land is a lake, bluer than this one here, and on that
lake, he told the wide-eyed Vogeli, was Ibarra, a city of ten
thousand inhabitants.

There, with one side fronting on the lake and the other on
the newly built railroad station, Goldoni would build him
a hotel, modern, complete from cellar to roof. It would have
no competition, since there was no other hotel, restaurant,
or café in the whole town. And he would never have to worry
about the steam heat—there was no need for any. It was
always pleasantly warm, not hot, not cold. It was, as he had
said before, the land of eternal spring.

Besides this, Goldoni explained, Vogeli would be a god.
"If you drive in a car," he told him, "and your hat blows
off, the policeman runs after it, and if he does not bring it
back quickly, you call him down and report him to his
superiors."

Vogeli then asked about butterflies. It was very late and
they went to the Café Saint Gotthard, because the Kursaal
closed at eleven, and there Goldoni continued his story and
ended by proposing a contract. Vogeli signed some papers,
sold his inn, packed, and left his wife, to go ahead to Ibarra.

"I found everything the way Goldoni had described it;
I must say that, I can't say different. The hotel was not
started yet, but the lake was there, a very beautiful lake.
The provisions are cheap here, and I can get all the employees I want for less than ten francs a month. No one
strikes in this country, and it rains very little. There isn't
another hotel or inn—that is true also. Ibarra has ten
thousand inhabitants, yes, but eight thousand of them are
children; the rest are Indians and have no money. There

are two white men, but they drive to Quito every week to eat and drink.

"But I like it here, I think I'll stay; I will look for a small place in Quito, and start with a pension. The butterflies amuse me, and they are a profitable hobby. I sell most of them.

"Besides, I can't go back. Everybody would hear about this, and the sparrows in Lucerne and Tribschen would whistle from the rooftops that Vogeli is a fool."

We walked back to the hotel. Painted over its door were a vine and some grapes. Vogeli pointed to them.

"Poor bird deceived with painted grapes," he sighed. In spite of his fine dog he wore a bracelet of fleabites; he scratched himself, and told me that the quotation was from Shakespeare.

21

The Friends of Ecuador.

Herr Vogeli, dressed in a green suit and a green hat, was standing first on one foot then on the other, looking around in all directions and saying that he could not wait any longer. "In this country you might as well throw your watch away. Nobody, not even the police are on time."

We had engaged a car for half-past seven, to take us back from Otavalo to Quito. It was now half-past eight. We walked through the town to look for it and it was nowhere to be seen.

At nine-thirty it appeared, an ancient Hupmobile. The driver explained that as soon as we had picked up another passenger, we could start, and he hoped that we had no objection to having somebody else ride along. The new passenger, he said, was a Government official. We sat down on a bench and waited, and for the next half-hour the Government official did not appear, so we asked the driver to take us to his house. It was half-past ten.

We drove to a little house and the driver honked his horn. The official came to the window in shirt and suspenders, and bowed and smiled, and lifted a finger as a signal. He disappeared between heavy white curtains, came back to the window a few seconds later, and held up a baby. Next the curtains were pushed aside by a fat round hand: a candy-colored satin bedjacket appeared, and Madame also nodded and smiled. There is nothing you can do when a baby is shown but nod and smile, and so Herr Vogeli smiled, the driver and his friend smiled, and I smiled.

The curtains closed, to open again in a little while; the

Government official continued the pantomime of the good life by showing us a coffee cup. He also signaled the fact that he was hurrying by gulping down a piece of bread. He bowed himself out, backing into the white curtains, and for the next ten minutes the window was dead. The door of the house opened about eleven and the official in black appeared, followed by wife and baby and a half-grown Indian girl who carried bottles, pillows, a rubber sheet, and a bag. All of them smiled and nodded; the baby cried and tried to swallow its small fist.

Herr Vogeli looked angry. The places were divided. It was a large car, with old upholstery, artificial flowers in small glass vases to left and right, and a rosary above the steering wheel.

It was eleven-thirty and we all sat up like sacks. The windows were half open but it smelled of nursery, of rubber sheet and boudoir, and of dog—the Saint Bernard was invisible, but unmistakably present, among the feet.

The chauffeur and his friend—drivers here always have a companion—were reasonably comfortable in front. The car started off and an animated conversation began in the front seat. The driver turned around, laughed, tried out a few English phrases, and pointed at the scenery. Only occasionally were both his hands on the wheel; sometimes he needed both of them to illustrate his conversation.

A few miles out of Otavalo, we came to the first blind and terrifying curve. It is a spot where you keep your mouth continually open to find words for the beauty of this land. We drove as fast as the car would go and on the wrong side of the road. Half a foot from the running board down to a mountain stream far below, stretched a prickly thicket of candelabra cacti and bayonet-leaved plants. To the right of the road was the base of another mountain that went straight up. On that side, in a small earthen niche, stood a statue of the Virgin. At her feet was an empty can that once had held tennis balls, now filled with field flowers, and the lower half of a beer bottle stuffed with a bouquet of forget-me-nots.

Just ahead in the middle of the road a four-year-old Indian girl in a blue poncho walked behind her sheep, and, squeezed against the bank, an Indian rode on his donkey. There was also a jet-black bull with wide horns, full grown, grazing on a thin strip of dusty grass.

Into this arrangement of animals and people, all so close that they touched each other, our car charged at full speed. The driver kept on laughing and talking to his friend even when an enormous bus appeared from the opposite direction. "Mamacita" was written on the sides of it. In the bus were some forty singing Indians, and on its roof, among clusters of bananas and chicken crates and sacks of corn, sat six more.

It was all over very quickly. Our driver took his hat off to the Madonna, the bus disappeared in a cloud of its own dust (it, too, had fortunately been on the wrong side of the road), the Virgin in her niche trembled a little, the bull cropped his grass, the little girl and her sheep went wandering on, the Indian on the donkey smiled and waved his hat. And it happened all over again on a curve a few miles farther on. God has not only made this country beautiful; He seems to close an eye very often in love for its people.

The mother, the baby, the nurse, and the dog were asleep. Herr Vogeli told the story of his experiences to the Government official and then he also fell asleep.

The official turned to me and observed that, while occasionally the immigrant is deceived, the Government has also had its share of painted grapes. He spoke of a group of Austrians that had come to Ecuador in 1928, a party of fifty men and fifty women. The opinion was then current, said the official, that foreigners had more business acumen, were braver, more resourceful, and enduring than the natives; and great concessions were made them.

The man who had organized the immigrants, a German, was well known in Quito. He was an adventurer who had lived several years in the jungles of the Oriente, and he had written many articles for an Austrian magazine called *Die Übersee Post*. In this paper he sang the usual praises of the rare woods, of gold and emeralds, the eternal spring and the flowers, and he mentioned the fact that eggs cost only one centavo apiece.

His articles got so much attention that he went to Vienna and organized a Society of the Friends of Ecuador. He issued membership pins and certificates, collected weekly dues, and accepted the savings of barbers, plumbers, chauffeurs, and store clerks. One farmer joined, too; and he sent them all to Ecuador.

He put one man in charge and he himself stayed behind to organize a second group.

On a cold and windy day in November, the first part of the Society of the Friends of Ecuador left Hamburg. They were miserable at first, and seasick, but after a while the cold wind stopped howling, the clouds moved away, the waters suddenly were blue and green. They had enough to eat and drink, and for the first time in their lives they were warm in winter. They lay on deck and let the sun shine on their pale stomachs, and all at once they were in Guayaquil.

They went to a small hotel. The one who was their spokesman wondered why no one had come to receive them. . . . They stayed in the small hotel until their money ran out; then they sat in the parks of Guayaquil. The authorities were up in Quito and knew nothing about them. The six policemen of Guayaquil looked upon white men as lords; they had never arrested a white man, and so they left them sitting in the parks unmolested.

The Government finally heard of them and took them to Riobamba and then to Quito. The fifty families were temporarily housed in the presidential quinta and a man was deputized to look after them. Every day they wrote on a piece of paper what they needed, including wine and beer, and it was given to them.

The Government then asked them to look around for land to settle on, and meanwhile granted them a pension of sixty sucres a month per person. The sucre at that time was four to the dollar.

It was arranged that the families should stay in Quito while the men went out to find farms. An additional grant was arranged to buy implements and seeds for them, once they had chosen their land.

The barbers, store clerks, and chauffeurs—and the one farmer—headed for the jungle, of which they had heard such wondrous tales. They found the orchids; the wild pigs came close to their camps; the forests were filled with game and the rivers with fish. The only unpleasant and disturb-

ing thing was the song of the ocelot at night: a noise like
that of a bow drawn slowly across a double bass. The men
hunted all day long and occasionally waded in the shallow
waters of the river to look for gold; each of them had a
horse, a saddle, a gun, a young Indian woman, and sixty
sucres for drink, and the eggs were really one centavo
apiece. They never wanted to go back.

There was loud howling from the wives and children left
in Quito, and finally the Government cut the pension; it
had had enough of them. The one farmer had cleared some
land and planted bananas, but the others went back. A few
left for Chile, others stayed in Quito to become barbers,
mechanics, and plumbers again; and one of them still works
in a butcher shop.—And that, said the Government official,
was the end of the Friends of Ecuador.

The silence that followed the story awakened the baby
and it was fed. Then all at once the car stopped, and the
radiator cap went up in a column of steam. The assistant
driver ran to a near-by brook and came back with water,
the car started and stopped again, and this time there was
no gas. . . .

The Government official looked at his watch and took the
baby, the Indian girl took the bottles and the rubber sheet,
and Herr Vogeli took the bag. We ran a little way to where
the track of the Quito–Esmeraldas Railroad crossed the
road and waited for the train. It stopped for the blue handkerchief which the Government official waved. Soon we were
all arranged in a first-class compartment, baby, rubber
sheet, dog, and all.

Herr Vogeli had put the official's bag in the baggage net
above his seat and had fallen asleep. For a while I debated

with myself whether I should wake him up or get up myself to push the little bag back. It slowly wobbled closer and closer to the edge of the baggage net and then began to lean over; it had almost gone too far when the train went up a a steep incline that made it slide back again into its proper place. Thus it advanced and retired several times, turning little by little, until it was flat against the wall and secure.

22

To a White Rose. Back at the

Hotel Metropolitano in Quito, I told the bellboys to have
the trunk sent to the railroad station and the bag to the
plane. Two boys carried the trunk out of the room. I had
never waited less than an hour for a car, half an hour for a
train, and I wondered whether the plane would leave on
time.

"They are gross and dull, these Germans, at times—God,
how dull they can be; but they are always orderly, and always on time," said André Roosevelt. "Look at Frau Ha-
gen: her house is in order, her husband is in order, and her
business is in order, and when we drive out to the flying field
you will see the motor going, gas and oil on board, and the
pilot ready."

We had to check the trunk through to Guayaquil first,
and we drove to the station. We overtook the trunk a few
blocks before we got there and saw that the bellboys had
farmed out the job. They were walking to the left and right
of the heavy trunk, and an Indian woman, quite an old one,
was carrying it on her back. The boys came along to col-
lect the tip.

The man in the baggage department was tired; he did
not weigh the trunk, he just walked around it. It was a
large wardrobe trunk and he pushed it a little, stood to one
side and crossed his arms, and then said, "Twenty sucres."

I said, "Oh, no, ten sucres."

Seventeen sucres it cost finally.

The plane was ready. It goes to Guayaquil in three-
quarters of an hour, the same distance which takes two days

in the train. There is no radio beam. Motor failure would
be fatal. Two German pilots are at the controls. They can't
carry much cargo, have to limit the number of passengers,
and take off with the gas tanks half full. The air up in
Quito is thin. The plane is an old Junkers Transport, but
they also have several smaller machines which are used for
charter flying and for surveying.

The pilots were young men; one of them had just arrived
from Germany, and the other was showing him the land-
marks along the route.

The plane, after rising from the field and circling it,
loses altitude until it is over the Guayas River. There it
banks and, tracing a half-circle over the cemetery, settles
on the field at Guayaquil. The field is surrounded by fences
and low wooden houses, with tall palm trees rising above
them and everywhere, on fences and roofs, no longer dis-
turbed by the roar of the engines, sit rows of black turkey
buzzards, silent and ominous.

I met Don Juan Palacios, my historian, in the lobby of
the Gran Hotel that evening. He sat next to an empty tea-
cup, under a sign that said, "Five o'clock tea, at all hours,"
and he almost burned his fingernails holding the stub of
a black, sweet-smelling Ecuadorian cigarette. He looked
more decayed than ever.

It was the beginning of the rainy season. The cloth of
my suit, the newspaper, my hat, everything was moist.
Sheets of water fell in the streets, small waterfalls ran off
the corners of buildings. And as soon as it stops raining a
plague of bugs arrives, and all at once they are everywhere;
their number is estimated in the millions. The bomberos are
called out sometimes with all their fire engines; they have to

wash the bugs off the sides of buildings, clear the telegraph poles, and flood them down the streets.

In the rest of the world they live out in the pantry, under the sink, and in the plumbing, and they are called cockroaches; but here they fly. They fly like swallows and they are worse than vultures, and on top of that they sing "Pyiiiiii, pyiiiiiiiii." Their name is "grillos." They love to eat cotton and wool. If they can't get either of these, they will take silk. I think that they know how to open doors and unlock trunks. Two of them can do away with a sweater in a few hours.

A grillo came gliding through the high portals of the hotel and—smack, bam!—landed on the glass-topped table in front of me. He folded his wings neatly under two covers and disappeared. Another one landed on my shoulder with the impact of someone slapping me.

"Sit still," said Don Juan, "the boy will take care of it."

A bellboy stationed there for this purpose came, and deftly threw the grillo to the tiled floor, where he spattered.

A whole group of them came flying in together. They settled on the floor, turned about as mechanical toys do, ran rapidly in this direction and that, feeling and tapping ahead continuously with long antennas. Six of them ran under a wicker chair and chased out a small, hysterical dachshund who had just arrived in Ecuador. His eyes glassy and his tail between his legs, he trembled and tried to get out of his collar. Don Juan Palacios bent down to the dog and assured him that the "cafards" would not eat him up.

"Oh, dear," said a woman at the left to her husband, introducing another woman, "I've just found out that we're

both from Mason City, Iowa. I want you to meet her. This
is Rose White——"

"Rose White"—Count de Ampurias turned in his chair,
looked at Rose White and translated the name, Rosa Blanca
—Rosa Blanca—Rosa Blanca. He played with the words,
and after a while he said, "Let's go along. I want you to
meet someone I am very fond of, an old friend of mine. I
want to take you to a very interesting place that you must
see before you leave Ecuador."

We took a car and drove to the old city, and then we
walked for a while. Majestic palms stood swaying among
rows of badly lit hovels. We walked through a melancholy
street without a sidewalk, without drainage; and I had to
grit my teeth because we slid along on a carpet of grillos.

The houses were of wood, and their doors of split bamboo. The only pieces of furniture in them were hammocks.
Through the open doors, in the rhythm of pendulums on
dozens of clocks, the feet of women were swinging from the
hammocks.

Stray donkeys and goats grazed on patches of grass between buildings and in the road; radios blared; there was
wild yelling, and the high hard voices of women. In front
of one house a man in a poncho was washing his hands in a
brook of water that ran down off the roof. At the end of the
slippery promenade, Don Juan Palacios loosened the grip
on my arm, pointed ahead, and said that this was where his
friend lived, the Villa Delicia.

"*Ah, mes belles années,*" he sighed. "She was as beautiful
as the Devil. Ah, when I was a young man, I wrote, I
danced, I played polo and piano. I don't shine at anything
much now."

We arrived at the gate of what was for this neighborhood
a reasonably permanent house. Every shutter was closed. It
stood in a garden with large trees, such as one finds in the
old cemetery in Guayaquil, and it must at one time have
been a good address.

For the last steps approaching the house, Don Juan
Palacios let go of my arm. He knocked loudly. A young
colored woman in a white apron opened the door, and when
we were inside, Don Juan said, "I wonder whether this is
the right house. I have not been here for years."

Just then a voice upstairs sang: "Amelia, *de l'eau
chaude—*" and the Count said, "Ah, yes, this is the place."

We walked into the parlor. Three chairs stood around a
table, and a buffet against the wall. As my eyes grew ac-
customed to the dim light in the room, I thought that I saw
a man looking up from under the buffet. I went and knelt
down, and saw the fat face of Charles Laughton. I looked
around the room then and discovered that it was papered
with a large poster for *Mutiny on the Bounty*.

The maid, who came in with some drinks, explained that
Doña Rosa was exceedingly fond of Clark Gable, and that
the local distributor for the films of several American companies, a friend of hers, had brought her the poster as a
gift. They had had much trouble finding a place where Mr.
Gable, full size, could be posted up to his best advantage.
The room was small and it was on this account that Charles
Laughton fared so badly. They had had to cut him in half
to fit the paper around a window. His head was near the
floor on one side of the room, and his legs and torso came
down from the ceiling opposite.

The agent had also sent a poster of the quintuplets, but

the maid informed us that Ecuador does not like quintuplets. There are too many children in Ecuador—children in Ecuador are nothing remarkable; to have five of them at once would be a catastrophe. Rosa Blanca, however, liked them, and she had cut them out and pasted them over the bed in the room where she slept. The maid opened another door, and we saw a brass bed in a blue room, with the quintuplets laughing down from the wall.

As the maid left the room, she was pushed aside by Rosa Blanca. Don Juan Palacios arose, and spread his arms, and muttered. There followed a vast exchange of caresses and mutual assurances of love and esteem. He kissed her hand and brought her across the room to introduce me.

She wore a yellow dress, tight and shiny like a wet lollipop. She was a comfortable bed of soft white flesh, her shoulders and bosoms the pillows and bolsters, her plump middle a plumeau. She had thick ears and a thick tongue and green eyes, and her hair, which was white at the roots for a sixteenth of an inch above her scalp, was a dead canary-yellow down to her shoulders.

She sat down and spoke of troubles with her hairdresser and of general ennui with the world. The Count moved close to her and kneaded her arm. With her free hand she toyed with a cross of garnets.

Don Juan shouted to the Negro girl for more beer, and he smoked several black cigarettes.

The cold wind that blows down into Guayaquil at night made the room uncomfortable, and Rosa Blanca sent the maid for her furs. A smeary silver-fox jacket was put across her shoulders.

The Count began to talk about the past. "Tw-tw-twenty

years ago," he started—and then he fell into a fit of cough-
ing, gulped like a fish, and suddenly looked like a corpse.

Rosa Blanca carried him onto the bed in the blue room,
and called to the maid to bring cold water. Then she tele-
phoned someone to come and fetch him home. She sat down
in the Mutiny on the Bounty room, looking warm and moist
and not without attraction. She belonged half in a salon and
half in a stable. She was a polyglot woman, speaking in four
languages at once. She did not like Ecuador, she said—no
concerts, no theater, nothing. The city she liked was Shanghai.

"In Shanghai, my friend in bed is also my friend on the
street. Here, if I meet him tomorrow on the street"—she
motioned with her head toward the blue room—"he will
pass me without seeing me. That is what I am going to have
put on my tombstone," she said. "*Vous qui passez sans me
voir*— I have to think up something to rhyme with that."

The Count sat up in bed and protested that it was not
true, what she had said; that he would not only recognize
her, but speak to her.

"Bah," she said, "go to sleep, lie down, quiet, sh!" But
Don Juan came to the door, like a child that refuses to go to
bed, and called her, "Rosa Blanca, Rosa Blanca, mon en-
fant, come here, come to me, my sweetheart."

He was in his stocking feet and his hair was disordered,
and he sagged at the knees. When he stood up straight, he
was about five feet two; now he was like a very old child.

"Go to bed, sh!" she said. Don Juan took out a diamond
stickpin and held it into the room under the lamp. Rosa
Blanca only said, "Go back to bed," and she went and
kissed him on the cheek. He jumped into bed with an unex-

pected leap. In the dark room he talked quietly to himself for a while until he fell asleep.

Rosa Blanca spoke of a son who was studying law in Santiago, Chile. She folded her large hands, which were not as clean as one might wish, in a peculiar fashion, a kind of interlocking of gears. Her fingers were covered with diamond rings as large as pieces of butter, all of them false. She talked of her husband, in the States, an impresario whose band was called the "Katz Embassy Grenadiers."

The housebell rang. A little man came for Don Juan Palacios, an earnest, insignificant, thin man, pale and worried, with a large nose. He was accompanied by a policeman, and he said neither "Good evening" as he came in, nor "Good night" as he left with his tired little brother.

23.

The S.S. *Santa Lucía.* "We

were not very serious last night," said Montegazza, when
he came to the hotel to see me off. He had a white rose
in the lapel of his *pet-en-l'air*. We crawled down the main
street of Guayaquil past the shops and had our shoes shined
and bought two lottery tickets.

When we came to a bookshop Don Palacios remembered
that he had promised to give me his history of Quito and a
set of his books on Ecuador. He lifted one foot and stepped
in and accosted a clerk with one of his imperial gestures. He
took the clerk aside and talked to him very earnestly.

The owner himself came out from under a stairway. He
bowed his greetings, and the three went into a corner where
there were many shelves of books.

Count de Ampurias took several thick leather-bound vol-
umes from the shelves and began stacking them together.
He opened one and commenced to read it. While the clerk
stayed beside him, the owner came and took me by the arm
and led me quietly over to the store's rear door. The Count
gave a quick look in my direction, a sudden signal of alarm
and suspicion, and returned to his book.

The owner said that it would be best if I left, or I would
never get rid of the old man. Don Juan Palacios, Count
de Ampurias y Montegazza, he explained, was not a count
at all. His real name was Cristóbal Calderón. He came of
an eminently respectable old family, was well-to-do, owned
a large hacienda—but had trouble inside his poor head.

He was not dangerous—"Oh, no, just peculiar." He
struck up friendships with visitors who interested him, and

appeared in curious outfits. When the exchange had been
better, he had lived all year in Paris; but now he was back
home.

The owner of the bookstore held the door open for me,
and said that the whole thing dated from very long ago, an
unhappy love affair. People said it had something to do
with roses. He bought roses, he wore roses, he looked up
every book on roses, and he raised them and sent them to
everybody he liked—white roses.

The proprietor opened the door a little wider and smiled
good-by. I said that I thought Count de Ampurias was a
very charming man. The proprietor closed the door.

"Ah, yes," he said, "and that is not all. He is noble, es-
teemed, very cultured and illustrious, and not sufficiently
celebrated—*nunco bien ponderado*."

With this threefold compliment we were back in the aisle
beside the Count, who took my arm and assured me that all
the books were ordered and would be sent to me directly to
New York. He turned and gave the bookseller some very
explicit shipping directions.

"*C'est ça*," he said.

The man bowed deeply and promised everything.

In slow advances, as if in oversized slippers, we walked
down to the Guayas River, and found the blue launch
Gloria—"the swiftest, the most commode, the most secure."
Her captain steered with his bare feet. A string of pelicans
came along in even beat, and they lifted themselves over the
roof of the small launch.

"Municipal councilors, we call them," said Montegazza,
"on account of the large mouth, the folds at the throat, and
the big belly."

He mounted the steps to the steamship one by one; to lift either of his legs some forty times was torture for him, and up on deck he sank into a chair in complete exhaustion. The last bananas were loaded below, the last passengers came aboard, two monkeys were sold and a lot of Panama hats. The Count had a drink with me, and when the whistle droned again, he left. The owner of the *Gloria* helped him down the ladder.

The little man became smaller and smaller and mixed into the people below. The blue launch *Gloria* pushed away. White cranes and blue herons sat in the trees along the riverbanks, and the drone of the *Santa Lucía's* steam whistle sent them up into the sky. The sailors on the battleship *C* waved good-by.

The land on both sides of the ship slipped away. Below in the launch Montegazza, his face the size and color of a walnut, waved his cane and his handkerchief, and over me came again the emotional sloppiness I feel when I go away from anywhere.

The *Santa Lucía* is like a big comfortable nurse. It is also like a country house. Everything is large and clean and orderly. The Captain's uniform is white and fits, and all the clocks are right. The pink ham and eggs look bright and clean and appetizing in the morning, and for dinner the ceiling rolls back and you can eat under the sky as on the roof of the Waldorf—with only the stars to show that the boat is moving.

Young girls in yellow dresses wait on you; there is no great formality. A slow and careful adjustment back to where trains run on time and bills are collected, to the sharp and serious life—an adjustment that is made very nicely.

The next morning, while we were still in Ecuadorian waters, I found near the swimming pool, beside a cup of coffee, an artificial leg. It was dressed in a tennis shoe, a white stocking, and a blue garter, and it remained there until lunch time. It was the last remnant of the beautiful madness of this lovely land.

AUTHOR'S NOTE

The Donkey Inside is the notebook or sketch-pad of several voyages through South America.

In a sense it is a portrait of that continent, from Chile to the Panama Canal, but it is focused on Ecuador, because there I found, in stronger outline than anywhere else, the things peculiar to South America.

Shielded by inadequate transportation (a small, baroque red train serves Quito three times a week, and it was not touched by airlines when I arrived), Ecuador has been left sleeping on, undisturbed by tourists.

The terrain, the architecture, and the landscape—the light that lies over it and the animals that walk about in it —are rendered as they are. As for the people, with the exception of André Roosevelt and his wife, the Indian boy Aurelio and all minor characters are wholly fictitious. Whenever character and person had to be painted in broad, immediate color, I have taken license to use the devices of the fiction writer. And to spare the reader the fatigue of meeting too many people, I have, whenever I found it right, put together several and of this amalgam made one person, such as Allan Ferguson. Cyril Vigoroux, for example, is a portrait of all the explorers I have met— at least of all the explorers of that type. I have taken the feet of one and the ears of another, and I hope it comes out all right.

Thus, too, it was actually three o'clock in the chapter where I make a boat arrive in the morning. The conversation with the Swiss hotelkeeper, on the train from Esmeraldas to Otavalo, really took place over the railing of a small steamer on the Lago de Todos Santos, in Chile.

It fitted so, it made a good picture.

Club Pichincha, Quito, Ecuador